STERLING BIOGRAPHIES

NEIL ARMSTRONG

One Giant Leap for Mankind

Tara Dixon-Engel & Mike Jackson

STERLING

New York / London
www.sterlingpublishing.com/kids

To Michael Engel, Katie Jackson, and Lori Jackson Zieg:
May you each find your wings and reach for the stars.

"Decide what you want to do, and never give up till you've done it."

STERLING and the distinctive Sterling logo are registered trademarks of
Sterling Publishing Co., Inc.

Library of Congress Cataloging-in-Publication Data

Dixon Engel, Tara.
  Neil Armstrong : one giant leap for mankind / by Tara Dixon-Engel & Mike Jackson.
    p. cm. — (Sterling biographies)
  ISBN-13: 978-1-4027-4496-9
  ISBN-10: 1-4027-4496-X
  1. Armstrong, Neil, 1930—-Juvenile literature. 2. Astronauts—United States—Biography—
Juvenile literature. I. Jackson, Mike, 1946- II. Title.

TL789.85.A75D59 2008
629.450092—dc22
[B]

2007048194

10 9 8 7 6 5 4 3 2 1

Published by Sterling Publishing Co., Inc.
387 Park Avenue South, New York, NY 10016

© 2008 by Tara Dixon-Engel & Mike Jackson

Distributed in Canada by Sterling Publishing
c/o Canadian Manda Group, 165 Dufferin Street
Toronto, Ontario, Canada M6K 3H6
Distributed in the United Kingdom by GMC Distribution Services
Castle Place, 166 High Street, Lewes, East Sussex, England BN7 1XU
Distributed in Australia by Capricorn Link (Australia) Pty. Ltd.
P.O. Box 704, Windsor, NSW 2756, Australia

Printed in China
All rights reserved

Sterling ISBN 978-1-4027-4496-9 (paperback)
Sterling ISBN 978-1-4027-6061-7 (hardcover)

For information about custom editions, special sales, premium and
corporate purchases, please contact Sterling Special Sales
Department at 800-805-5489 or specialsales@sterlingpublishing.com.

Designed by Erica Kalish for SimonSays Design!
Image research by Larry Schwartz

Contents

Events in the Life of Neil Armstrong

1930

August 5, 1930
Neil Armstrong is born in Wapakoneta, Ohio.

August 5, 1946
Neil turns sixteen and earns his pilot's license.

October 14, 1947
Chuck Yeager breaks the sound barrier, paving the way for the space program.

June 7, 1950
Armstrong makes his first carrier landing on the USS *Essex*.

1955
Armstrong becomes a research pilot for NASA's Lewis Center (now the Glenn Center) in Cleveland, Ohio. Later that same year, he transfers to Edwards Air Force Base in California.

June 30, 1957
Eric "Ricky" Armstrong is born.

October 7, 1958
NASA launches Project Mercury, its first human-in-space program.

September 17, 1962
Stephen and Viola Armstrong announce on national television, "Our son became an astronaut today."

April 8, 1963
Mark Armstrong is born.

Jan. 27, 1967
The crew of *Apollo 1* are killed in a launchpad fire at Cape Canaveral.

April 14, 1969
NASA announces that Armstrong will command *Apollo 11*.

July 20, 1969
Neil Alden Armstrong becomes the first human to set foot on the moon.

August 1971
Armstrong resigns from NASA and accepts a teaching position at the University of Cincinnati.

1994
Armstrong marries Carol Knight.

1937
Neil takes his first airplane ride in a Ford Tri-Motor Tin Goose.

September 1947
Armstrong begins college at Purdue University through a naval aviation scholarship.

1950
Armstrong is called up by the navy for the Korean conflict.

September 3, 1951
Armstrong's plane is struck by enemy fire over Korea; he ejects over the Sea of Japan.

January 28, 1956
Neil Armstrong and Janet Shearon are married.

October 4, 1957
The Russians launch Sputnik, the first human-made satellite to orbit the Earth.

April 13, 1959
Karen Anne "Muffie" Armstrong is born.

January 28, 1962
Karen Anne dies of a brain tumor at age three.

March 16, 1966
Neil Armstrong's first spaceflight, *Gemini VIII*, is launched.

December 21, 1968
Apollo 8 makes an unprecedented flight to the moon. They orbit the moon and prove that humans can travel there and back safely.

July 16, 1969
Apollo 11 launches.

July 24, 1969
Apollo 11 safely returns to Earth, splashing down in the Pacific Ocean.

1989
Neil and Jan divorce.

2005
The first authorized biography of Neil Armstrong, *First Man*, is released.

From Fiction to Reality

We came in peace for all mankind.

—Plaque left on the moon

On July 20, 1969, the smooth blackness of space was broken by a spidery silver machine that dropped slowly toward the gray powdery surface of the moon. At a distance, it might have been mistaken for a child's toy, molded from paper clips, tin cans, and scraps of aluminum foil. Close up, the odd little spacecraft was a miracle of modern technology, and a testament to American initiative and determination.

It was a scene that had been played out countless times in hundreds of science-fiction tales over the years. But suddenly it was no longer the stuff of fiction. This was reality. Men from Earth were about to set foot on the surface of the moon.

Our fascination with the moon is as old as humankind itself. Since the dawn of time, we have scanned the night sky wondering about the milky white globe that chased away the sun at day's end.

Now a shy, yet driven young man from Ohio named Neil Armstrong was about to discover its secrets. As commander of *Apollo 11*, he and his crew had traveled thousands of miles to get to this point in the solar system. No one ever doubted that Neil would leave his mark in *this* world, but few could have predicted that he would leave his mark on the powdery surface beyond our world as well.

CHAPTER 1

Beautiful Ohio

He thinks, he acts, 'tis done.

—*Neil Armstrong's high school yearbook*

Long before he rode a rocket to the moon, Neil Alden Armstrong was a young boy growing up in rural Ohio. Born on August 5, 1930, in Wapakoneta, Neil was the eldest child of Stephen Koenig Armstrong and Viola Louise Engel Armstrong.

When Neil was three years old his sister, June, was born. His brother, Dean, came along almost two years later.

Neil was born at the beginning of America's Great Depression. It was a time of hardship and unemployment for millions of people. In the worst situations, people had to beg on street corners to get food and money. The Armstrongs were fortunate that Stephen had a marketable

America's Great Depression lasted from 1929 to 1939; more than fifteen million people were jobless. Neil's father had steady work, however, so the Armstrongs had no need of the breadlines or soup kitchens that sprang up across the country, as shown in this 1930 photograph.

skill and was a good provider. As an auditor of county records for the state of Ohio, his job was to go through county financial reports and make sure they were accurate. He would study the books for almost a year and then move on to the next county. This meant that the family moved frequently, but there was always a roof over their heads and food on the table. Young Neil barely had time to make friends before he was back on the road again and headed toward a new community.

Like most mothers in the 1930s, Viola Armstrong was a homemaker. She spent a great deal of time reading to her children and nurturing their interest in music and books.

Airplanes and the mechanics of flight captured Neil's attention at a very young age. In 1936, Stephen Armstrong surprised his son Neil with a Sunday-morning visit to a local airport where a pilot was offering discounted airplane rides. Just ten days shy of his sixth birthday, the young adventurer climbed into a Ford Tri-Motor airplane in Warren, Ohio, and enjoyed his first trip skyward. The old Ford Tri-Motor was also known as the Tin Goose because it was metal and quite loud as it chugged across the sky. Stephen Armstrong acknowledged that he was a bit uneasy during the flight, but young Neil took to it immediately.

In later years, however, Neil would admit that he had no memory of the Tin Goose flight, nor of his parents taking him to watch the Cleveland Air Races. Memory or not, these events surely planted a seed, one that would sink its roots deep into young Neil's character and ambition.

Neil's first airplane ride was on a Ford Tri-Motor, affectionately nicknamed the Tin Goose.

The Ford Tri-Motor

The Ford Tri-Motor was a three-engine civilian airplane that was first produced by the Ford Motor Company in the mid-1920s. Between 1925 and 1933, about two hundred of the Tri-Motors were built by Ford. The aircraft was nicknamed the Tin Goose or Flying Washboard because of its all-metal construction. It was the first plane built for passenger travel, rather than mail delivery, and could fly higher and faster than other aircraft of that era. The Tri-Motor could fly up to 130 miles per hour and had seating for up to eight people.

In November 1929, famed navigator Admiral Richard Byrd and pilot Bernt Balchen trusted the sturdy little Tin Goose to take them safely over the South Pole. It was the first flight ever over this frozen and desolate stretch of land, taking the adventurers eighteen hours and thirty-nine minutes to complete.

Explorer Richard Byrd and pilot Bernt Balchen successfully piloted a Tin Goose on the first-ever flight over the South Pole.

An Early Passion for Aviation

By the age of eight, Neil was building model airplanes out of paper and balsa wood. Each model cost him about ten cents to build. He spent long hours carefully assembling the fliers, surely dreaming that one day he, too, would control the dips and turns of a powerful airplane. Neil's passion for aviation became so consuming that he eventually constructed a small wind tunnel in the basement of the family's home. There he could test the **aerodynamics** of his model planes and determine the best design for the highest, fastest, and farthest flight.

"It was a fun project. I blew out of a lot of fuses in my home," Neil recalled, chuckling. "Because I tried to build a rheostat [a controller] that would allow the electric motor to change speed and then get various air flows through the tunnel . . . not altogether successfully."

He didn't know it at the time, but Neil was taking the first steps toward becoming a test pilot, one of the most dangerous—and exciting— professions in the world.

As a boy, Neil delighted in building model airplanes like the one shown here.

Working to Finance His Interests

By the time Neil turned ten, his family was living in Upper Sandusky, Ohio, having moved from Cleveland, Warren, Jefferson, and St. Mary's following his birth in Wapakoneta.

Wind Tunnels

A wind tunnel is a cylinder that has air blowing through it. The first ones were built back in 1871. Scientists or designers place a test object (often a wing or a model airplane) in the test section of the tunnel. By observing how the air blows over the object—and the forces and pressure this creates—scientists can improve the test item's shape and design in order to make an airplane fly better or faster.

This 1931 wind tunnel allowed aircraft designers to test the impact of airflow over the control surfaces of an airplane.

A wind tunnel can be as big as a football field or so small that you can carry it from room to room. Although most wind tunnels are horizontal (the air flows from side to side), vertical wind tunnels (with the air blowing upward) are also used to allow skydivers to practice their techniques.

His passion for model airplanes continued to thrive. America was still struggling to recover from a global economic depression, and money was scarce. Neil's parents did not hand him money for every project or interest; instead, they required that their children earn the money for their activities and hobbies. Neil paid for his hobby by taking a job mowing grass at a local cemetery.

Neil was small for his age, and his size is likely what earned him his next job at Neumeister's Bakery, where he was able to shimmy into the mixing vats and clean them. Because of his mother's early influence, Neil's passion for aviation was joined with a love of music. His work at Neumeister's allowed him to earn the money necessary to buy a baritone horn so he could join the school band.

Neil would enjoy playing the baritone well into his college years. In fact, to this day the Purdue University Marching Band proudly notes that it's the only band in the world with the distinction of having once featured a young musician who would become the first human to set foot on the moon.

While still in Upper Sandusky, Neil became a charter member of a new Boy Scout troop there. With his friends Konstantine "Kotcho" Solacoff and John "Bud" Blackford, Neil began pursuing his Tenderfoot badge in Troop 25. Neil's many interests and activities sometimes threatened to overwhelm him, as on the day of the troop's twenty-five-mile hike. Neil and his pals made the hike to fulfill the requirements of his Hiking merit badge, but after twenty-two miles, young Armstrong realized that he was going to be late for his job at the bakery. So he ran much of the next three miles to get to Neumeister's, where he worked until eleven o'clock that night! Such determination and commitment eventually earned Neil the highest rank in Scouting, that of Eagle Scout.

Neil was a Boy Scout and achieved the highest rank in Scouting, that of Eagle Scout. A Boy Scout from 1938—approximately the time Neil was also a scout—is pictured above.

In later years, Bud Blackford would credit the Boy Scouts with shaping Neil's personality and giving him the tools to pursue and achieve his goals.

Armstrong's High School Days

During Neil's first year of high school, Stephen Armstrong changed jobs again, moving from the auditor's office to the department of public welfare. The family moved back to Wapakoneta, where Neil's grandparents owned a farm just outside town.

As a sophomore at Blume High School, Neil was active in the band, glee club, and student council, earning a reputation as a go-getter whose quiet demeanor didn't stand in the way of achieving his goals. In his high school yearbook, classmates paid tribute to his thoughtful, methodical approach to life by placing the following quote next to his name: "He thinks, he acts, 'tis done."

NEIL A. ARMSTRONG
"He thinks, he acts, 'tis done."

Band 2, 3, 4, Vice-President 4; Orchestra 3; Glee Club 2; Student Council 3, 4, Vice-President 4; Retrospect Staff; Junior Hi-Y 2; Senior Hi-Y 3, 4; Boosters Club 2, 3, 4, Junior Class Play; Home Room President 3; Boys' State 3; Transferred from Upper Sandusky High School 1.

Neil's high school yearbook photo also carries a commentary about him: "He thinks, he acts, 'tis done."

A Young Pilot

That quote could also be applied to the young man's passion for flight. By the age of fifteen, when most teenage boys were anticipating that rite of passage known as a driver's license, young Armstrong set his sights higher . . . literally. Working a variety of jobs in Wapakoneta, the would-be aviator earned enough money for flying lessons at a local airport. The plane he trained in was an Aeronca Champ, a snazzy little two-seater with a frontseat/backseat configuration that packed only sixty-five

The Aeronca Champ, originally produced in Middletown, Ohio, gave Neil his first taste of flight and independence. At sixteen, he earned his private pilot's license.

horsepower, allowing it to fly not much faster than the average car! Then again, you couldn't do steep turns, stalls, and spins in the average car.

For a young pilot eager to test his wings, the Champ offered challenge and satisfaction as Armstrong maneuvered the stick and throttle while peering out over the nose of the aircraft. During those first flights, the Champ gave him confidence and an exhilarating sense that he was practically sitting astride the nose, watching the landscape glide past. It was invigorating and habit forming.

But flying lessons, even then, weren't cheap. At nine dollars an hour, Armstrong had to work more than twenty hours for one lesson. And that didn't count paying for his flying magazines, his model airplanes, and all the normal activities that occupy the attention and energy of teenage boys.

In addition to savoring his time in the air, Armstrong was fascinated by the activity in and around the airport itself. He soon became a "**hangar** rat," haunting the grounds in search of odd jobs and any chance to tinker with the inner workings of an airplane. Like many young pilots, Armstrong didn't simply want to fly the airplanes; he wanted to understand them, inside and out!

Shortly after he began his flight training, Armstrong got his first close-up look at the place where his flights would eventually take him—the moon. A neighbor by the name of Jacob Zint was an amateur **astronomer** and had set up a telescope on his garage roof. Neil and his pals trooped over there one evening to view a meteor shower. It was the beginning of many visits to the roof for the young pilot. Zint recalled that Neil spent a great deal of time looking at the moon and would often speculate on the likelihood of life on other planets.

Like many young pilots, Armstrong didn't simply want to fly the airplanes; he wanted to understand them, inside and out!

On August 5, 1946, Neil celebrated his sixteenth birthday with a very special present to himself—a pilot's license. Although he couldn't drive a car yet, young Neil Armstrong could soar above the Earth all by himself and marvel at the rolling Ohio landscape beneath him.

CHAPTER 2

A Flying Boilermaker

*[A] good landing [is] one you can walk away from.
[An] excellent landing [is] one you can walk away
from, and use the same airplane twenty-four hours
after landing.*

— Old pilot's saying

Neil Armstrong knew that he wanted to go to college. He also knew that his career of choice was aeronautical engineering—the scientific study of the design and construction of aircraft. After all, what with his model airplanes, his homemade wind tunnel, and his actual flying experience, he was already an expert in the making!

Neil's family, while not poor, was also not rich enough to send him to college. He had saved some money from his numerous part-time jobs, but not enough to cover the cost of a four-year degree. Armstrong knew he was going to need some financial support. He read about scholarships being offered through the U.S. Naval Aviation College Program, which allowed students to attend any four-year college accredited by the navy, in exchange for three years of naval service.

This photo shows the south side of the Purdue University campus, where Neil received a degree in aeronautical engineering.

Following a two-day qualifying test in Cincinnati, Armstrong was notified that he had been awarded a scholarship and could attend the college of his choice. All his teachers urged him to select Purdue University in West Lafayette, Indiana, because of its highly regarded aeronautical engineering program. Neil did just that, and in the autumn of 1947 he and his parents made the 150-mile drive to Purdue. He was now officially a "Boilermaker"—the Purdue mascot nickname.

Called to Active Duty

Armstrong quickly fell into the rhythm of college life, but he only had three semesters under his belt when the navy called him up for active duty in 1949. He was sent to naval flight school in Pensacola, Florida. There he received instruction in one of the most famous training aircraft of World War II, the SNJ—also known as the T-6 Texan. Armstrong struggled with some aspects of flying the T-6, earning himself numerous ratings of below average and unsatisfactory on elements such as taxiing ("driving" the plane across the ground), landing the plane, and maintaining its altitude in case of an emergency. Despite some rocky moments, Armstrong's instructors soon began to view him as a skilled pilot, and ratings of average and above average soon outnumbered his scores of unsatisfactory and below average.

Neil took his flight training in a navy SNJ aircraft, also known as the T-6 Texan, like those shown here at Randolph Field in 1941.

While Armstrong was completing his training as a naval aviator, the Korean War broke out in 1950, and the young Ohioan was called on to serve in Fighter Squadron 51 (VF-51), an all-jet unit stationed in California. At twenty, Neil Armstrong was the youngest member of the squadron, but that didn't stop him from being assigned to the USS *Essex* aircraft carrier, where he would learn to master one of the most difficult challenges for a fighter pilot—carrier takeoffs and landings.

Carrier Landings

Landing on the flight deck of an aircraft carrier is a tough job for even the most experienced navy pilot. The flight deck only has about five hundred feet of runway space, which isn't nearly enough for today's fast, heavy aircraft. As a result, navy aircraft are equipped with a tail hook, a long hook attached to the plane's tail. To make a safe carrier landing, the pilot must catch the tail hook on one of four arresting cables made of high-tensile steel wire. The arresting wires stretch across the deck about fifty feet apart, attached to hydraulic cylinders below decks. The arresting wire can stop a fifty-four-thousand-pound aircraft traveling 150 miles per hour in only two seconds, in a 315-foot landing area. A pilot hopes to snag the third wire, because it's in the safest position. The first wire is too close to the front edge of the deck. The second or fourth wire is acceptable. But a proficient naval aviator prides himself on grabbing the third wire every time.

Carrier landings are some of the toughest maneuvers in aviation. Here, an F9F Panther jet catches the arresting wire aboard the USS *Oriskany*.

Six months after joining VF-51, Neil Armstrong would make his first carrier landing on the *Essex* on June 7, 1950. It was a significant moment for the young pilot, one he would later describe as "a very emotional achievement." There is a saying in aviation that a "good landing [is] one you can walk away from. [An] excellent landing [is] one you can walk away from, and use the same airplane twenty-four hours after landing."

For carrier landings, no truer words were ever spoken. Just learning to land a plane skillfully is complicated, but landing it on a tiny runway that's bobbing up and down—and moving forward at the same time—is a challenge that leaves even experienced pilots weak in the knees. Armstrong's carrier landings were all successful though, earning him eight ratings of average and only two of below average. That same week, he would advance from the rank of **midshipman** to **ensign**. By the end of the month, Armstrong and the *Essex* were headed for Korea, where VF-51 jets would serve as ground attack aircraft.

The USS *Essex*, pictured here in 2007, is an example of a modern aircraft carrier.

Crippled in Midair

Armstrong's first encounter with the enemy took place on August 29, 1951, while he was flying an F9F Panther, serving as escort for a **photo reconnaissance** lane over Songjin, Korea. Five days later, Armstrong and his Panther were struck by anti-aircraft fire during a low bombing run over a freight yard and bridge south of the village of Majon-ni, west of Wonsan. The shell fragments, known as shrapnel, tore away about six feet of Armstrong's right wing, leaving him able to limp the aircraft back to friendly territory, but unable to land it.

So the young pilot had to make a decision he hoped to never make again—he had to eject from the damaged aircraft. For any pilot, ejection is always the last option. Naturally, there is a certain pilot bravado that says, I can fly any plane safely home, no matter how badly damaged it is. But beyond the desire for bragging rights is the pilot's knowledge that ejection is terribly dangerous. Weather conditions, winds, mechanical problems, the condition of the aircraft, and numerous other factors can often make it safer to stay with a crippled plane. Also, ejection is a violent act that can lead to spinal injuries.

Still, Neil knew that the **aileron** had been ripped from his wing and he could never make a controlled landing. "The plane's control system was knocked out," he would later recall. "I could stay in the air, but I couldn't land."

Ejection was the safest of several risky options. The young flier opted to try to eject over the Sea of Japan, where he figured he could tread water until navy helicopters fished him out. Flying to an airfield near P'ohang, he bailed out of the plane, only to encounter winds that buffeted his parachute back over land. Luckily, the young ensign survived his hard landing and was picked up in a jeep driven by one of his flight school roommates.

Armstrong's battered airplane was never recovered and likely did a swan dive into the Sea of Japan, where it settled into a watery grave.

Ejection Seats

The ejection process is violent and unpredictable. Pictured here is an Air Force Thunderbirds pilot ejecting from a jet traveling approximately 250 miles per hour. The pilot survived this ejection, but the aircraft crashed into the runway and exploded.

Most military jets have ejection seats, which allow pilots to leave the cockpit quickly in the event of an emergency. While ejecting can sometimes save a pilot's life, it carries its own set of dangers, and most pilots prefer to try to land the plane, rather than risking life and limb through ejection. In most designs, an explosive charge blasts the canopy off the jet and propels the seat into the air and (hopefully) away from the aircraft. A parachute then deploys, and a seat-separation mechanism separates the pilot from his perch, allowing him to float safely to Earth. The purpose of an ejection seat is to save the pilot's life, but many fliers have sustained permanent injury in the process. During ejection, the body is subjected to more than fourteen g's of pressure (fourteen times the weight of his or her body). With older ejection seats, pilots often endured up to twenty-two g's. No matter how technology has improved the ejection process, all pilots prefer to return to Earth the same way they left it . . . in a functional aircraft!

Armstrong would eventually fly a total of seventy-eight missions during the Korean War, for a total of 121 hours of combat flying, much of which took place in January 1952. For his service to America, Neil Armstrong was presented the Air Medal for twenty combat missions, a gold star for the next twenty, and the Korean Service Medal and engagement star. He left the navy on August 23, 1952, becoming a lieutenant, junior grade, in the U.S. Naval Reserve. He would eventually resign his commission in the naval reserve on October 20, 1960.

Returning to Purdue

In the fall of 1952, at the age of twenty-two, Armstrong returned to Purdue to complete his interrupted college education. Once again he settled into a routine, joining the band, the aero club, Phi Delta Theta fraternity, and—in a preview of things to come—the American Rocket Society, an organization

Janet Shearon, who would become Mrs. Neil Armstrong, pictured here in 1956.

promoting the exploration of space. Who could have known that the club's quiet, sandy-haired new member would one day make history's most significant contribution to space exploration?

Always a hard worker, Armstrong began a daily newspaper route that took him across campus during the wee hours of the morning. It was during those morning jaunts that he met a young coed heading for her 7 a.m. home economics lab. Janet Shearon was a native of Evanston, Illinois, who appreciated Armstrong's quiet, methodical nature as well as his interest in aviation. The two became friends but did not date each other right away. "He is not one to rush into anything," Jan told *Life* magazine many years later. In late 1955, he made up his mind that Jan needed to change her name to Armstrong. The couple was married on January 28, 1956.

CHAPTER 3

Higher, Faster, Farther

I knew him . . . but I didn't know him.
  —Milt Thompson, a fellow aviator

After graduating from Purdue in 1955 with his degree in aeronautical engineering, Armstrong had joined the National Advisory Committee for Aeronautics (NACA) as a research pilot. At the age of twenty-four, he began work at the Lewis Flight Propulsion Laboratory (now the Glenn Research Center) in Cleveland, Ohio. As a research pilot, Armstrong's job was not simply to test aircraft but also to help push the limits of aviation science and technology—to find new answers to old questions, and to raise new questions with no answers—yet.

Moving to California

Though Neil was working in his home state, his heart was urging him toward Edwards Air Force Base in California, where so many of the cutting-edge, high-speed flight test initiatives were taking place. Less than ten years earlier, a hotshot air force jet jockey named Chuck Yeager had shattered the sound barrier in the skies over California, paving the way for serious inroads into space travel research.

Edwards, formerly known as the Muroc Army Airfield, sprawled across several dry lakebeds in Antelope Valley. Despite the lush backdrop of the San Gabriel Mountains, the base itself was flat, dry, and hot. But each

One of the most famous test pilots ever, Chuck Yeager, stands next to the Bell X-1 in which he broke the sound barrier on October 14, 1947.

morning brought the kind of still, clear air that inspired euphoria in pilots. Such conditions were ideal for testing the limits of a high-performance aircraft's endurance and **maneuverability**. The desert stillness was often short-lived, as the sound of revving jet engines broke the calm, followed shortly by the boom of exotic aircraft smashing the sound barrier. It was a test pilot's answer to heaven on Earth, and Armstrong wanted to be in the thick of it.

Fortunately, Armstrong only had to wait a few months before the call came offering him the job of his dreams. He was heading to California and right into the exciting, dangerous world of test flying at its seat-of-the-pants best!

Then, in 1957, Neil and Jan became the parents of Eric Alan, whom they quickly nicknamed Ricky. Neil savored this time with his new family, even as he threw himself into the detailed research and analysis that was the trademark of the NACA test program.

The Race for Space

Many things were happening in the world—and out of it— that were pushing America to push its pilots and its aircraft designers. In October 1957, Armstrong and the rest of the country had been caught by surprise when the Russians launched the first human-made satellite into space.

Chuck Yeager and the Sound Barrier

Air force test pilot Captain Charles "Chuck" Yeager was selected by NACA to fly the rocket-powered Bell X-1 to research the potential of high-speed flight and, specifically, to break the sound barrier. There was great danger associated with this mission. But what was the sound barrier—and why did pilots fear it?

The sound barrier is the point at which an object moves faster than the speed of sound—roughly 769 miles per hour. It never was a "barrier"—although many pilots viewed it as such. As an aircraft approaches the speed of sound, it encounters turbulence and a variety of changes in air pressure, temperature, and density. Early jet design did not take these factors into consideration, and as a result aircraft vibrated themselves to pieces, leading some to conclude that they were hitting an invisible wall in the sky.

Today planes routinely exceed the speed of sound, which is identified by "Mach" numbers (Mach 1 being the speed of sound, Mach 2 twice the speed of sound, and so forth). Yeager flew the Bell X-1 to Mach 1.06 at forty-three thousand feet on October 14, 1947. He did so with two cracked ribs, courtesy of a horseback-riding accident two days earlier. The "breaking" of the sound barrier creates an explosive noise called a sonic boom.

The Bell X-1 prepares to break the sound barrier over Muroc Army Airfield (later known as Edwards Air Force Base) in 1951.

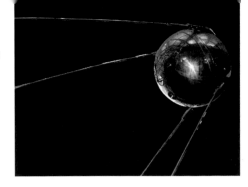

Sputnik, this beeping sphere launched by the Russians in October 1957, was the first satellite of its kind.

This metallic, beeping sphere was nicknamed Sputnik by the Russians (known then as the Soviet Union or the USSR—Union of Soviet Socialist Republics). The translation of the word *sputnik*—"little traveler"—seemed pretty harmless, but the implications of the Soviet Union having an "eye in the sky" were anything but.

America was locked in a Cold War with the Soviet Union. The two countries had completely different political and economic beliefs, and each viewed the other as a potential opponent in nuclear war. When Soviet premier Nikita Khrushchev told Westerners, "We will bury you," Americans had good reason to fear this sprawling and determined superpower.

Sputnik quickly coaxed America's behind-the-scenes air and space research out into the open. By 1958, NACA had been rechristened NASA—the National Aeronautics and Space Administration—and the organization was moving full-tilt toward something big. The space race was on.

Nikita Khrushchev, leader of the Union of Soviet Socialist Republics, listens to the General Assembly at the United Nations in 1960.

The Space Race

The space race was really a lengthy "battle" in the Cold War. The United States and the Soviet Union pitted their technology and know-how against each other in order to achieve a definitive goal: putting the first man on the moon. The Russians were early favorites to win this particular contest. They launched the first human-made satellite. They launched the first man, Yuri Gagarin, into space. But on May 25, 1961, President John F. Kennedy made space exploration a national priority and urged Americans to take up the cause. During an address before Congress, Kennedy said, "I believe that this nation should commit itself to achieving the goal, before this decade is out, of landing a man on the moon and returning him safely to the earth. No single space project in

this period will be more impressive to mankind, or more important for the long-range exploration of space; and none will be so difficult or expensive to accomplish." Although Kennedy would not live to see his challenge met, he inspired nationwide resolve to beat the Russians to the surface of the moon.

In May 1961, President John F. Kennedy addresses a joint session of Congress and lays out his plan to put an American on the moon and return him safely to Earth.

While NACA had focused on advancing our nation's aeronautical technology within Earth's atmosphere, NASA was looking beyond the horizon, way beyond. The new agency would be adding space-related research and development to its list of priorities. Shortly after changing its name and its mission, NASA would begin interviewing and testing pilots from across the country—the best of the best—for a new and dangerous assignment. NASA was on the hunt for astronauts!

What Was an Astronaut?

What exactly was an astronaut? Armstrong and many others wondered. Well, NASA wasn't entirely sure, either—mainly because the space agency didn't fully know what might be required of these fly boys who would hopefully lead America into space. No one really understood what the stresses of space travel would do to the human body. How would it react to weightlessness? To intense **g-forces**? To the searing heat of reentry into the Earth's atmosphere from space? How would these fliers react emotionally to danger, isolation, and extreme conditions?

There were medical doctors who firmly believed that weightlessness would cause an individual's heart and lungs to explode—or that the loneliness of space travel would drive a person insane! As a result of all the uncertainty, NASA tested its potential astronauts in ways that would startle, embarrass, and press them to the limits of their physical and mental endurance.

The final thirty-two astronaut candidates for phase one of the space program were tested from head to toe on the functioning of their ears, eyes, nose, mouth, brain, muscles, nerves, heart, lungs, bowels, blood flow, and emotional/mental endurance. They were stabbed with needles, set on treadmills, deprived of sleep, and forced to sit naked on blocks of ice! They were hooked

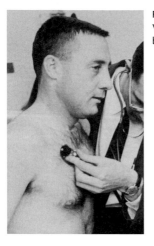
Physical exams are a way of life for an astronaut. Virgil "Gus" Grissom is pictured here being examined by a NASA physician.

up to machines that jolted them with electrical shocks, causing their muscles to ball up into painful knots. They were subjected to humiliating interviews and forced to write papers answering questions such as "Who am I?" and "Whom would you assign to the mission if you could not go yourself?"

It was a grueling process that later astronauts would gratefully be spared. Some rebelled in subtle ways. Among the group of initial potential astronauts, a young navy pilot named Pete Conrad, known for his smart mouth and his tongue-in-cheek philosophy of "if you can't be good, be colorful," soon tired of all the tests and questions. When a NASA psychologist showed him a blank sheet of paper and asked, "What do you see," Conrad studied it carefully before explaining to the "shrink" with mock seriousness that he couldn't really tell because the picture was upside down. Such impudence may have weeded Pete out of the first group of astronauts, but he would eventually get his time in space as the commander of the *Apollo 12* mission and the third man on the moon. Even there, Pete found ironic humor as he dubbed his mission "history's ultimate also-ran."

But when all the initial tests were finished and all the candidates were sized up, NASA

Pete Conrad, who entered the astronaut corps along with Neil, was arguably one of the most colorful and entertaining astronauts in the early space program.

Military pilots all, the Mercury Seven pose for a NASA publicity shot. From the left: Scott Carpenter, navy; Gordon Cooper, air force; John Glenn, marines; Gus Grissom, air force; Wally Schirra, navy; Alan Shepard, navy; and Deke Slayton, air force.

selected seven "ordinary supermen" to trot out before the media as the world's first astronauts, known as the Mercury Seven.

A Stickler for Privacy

In 1958, however, the space agency was still gearing up for the next two years of change and challenge. Young Neil Armstrong was not yet interested in being either an astronaut or an astronaut candidate. He was just happy to be living out the test pilot's credo of *Higher, faster, and farther* on a daily basis.

Armstrong quickly earned a reputation at Edwards as a brilliant engineer—and as someone who carefully guarded everything he did and said. His deep and abiding shyness was sometimes mistaken for arrogance or aloofness. He was fiercely protective of his privacy and was never one to engage in idle chitchat. Everything he did and said seemed to have a purpose behind it. Milt Thompson, one of his fellow pilots at NACA, would later comment that "I knew him . . . but I didn't know him."

Armstrong had a quiet determination and a distrust of strangers outside his "clan" or circle of intimate family and friends.

As if to underscore the need for privacy, he and Jan, who had not been in California very long, decided to buy a cabin nestled a few thousand feet up in the San Gabriel Mountains. There was no electricity and no hot water. Neil had the luxury of traveling into the high-tech world of Edwards Air Force Base every day, leaving Jan to deal with the challenges of raising a young son in the midst of some difficult conditions. When she wanted to bathe Ricky, she would fill up a tub with cold water and set it out in the sun to warm. She would occasionally wander out into the yard to watch her husband's test plane streak across the California sky.

When he wasn't flying state-of-the-art aircraft, Armstrong worked to upgrade the cabin where he and Jan lived. Ever independent, he would not hire others to do his renovations, but relied on do-it-yourself guides to home improvement.

A Passion for Gliding

It's safe to say that Armstrong cherished flight, silence, and individual challenge. So it was appropriate that he would develop a fascination with gliders and soaring. The heated soil of Edwards and the Antelope Valley provided the perfect environment for soaring, where columns of warm air could keep an unpowered aircraft, known as a glider, aloft.

Armstrong described the sport of gliding as "very demanding," adding that "you can't blame the mistakes on anyone but yourself." While he loved to press his aviation skills to the limit, he avoided risking the lives of others in the process.

He had applied a similar logic to his desire to fly single-seat fighters in the navy, reasoning that any mistakes or miscalculations on his part would not endanger anyone but himself.

Gliders

A glider offers a challenge to its pilot, who must stay aloft by catching the lifting power of "thermals" radiating up from Earth's surface.

Gliders were among the earliest aircraft, dating back to the eighteenth century and perhaps before. The Wright brothers, Wilbur and Orville, experimented with gliders in order to prove their theories on flight. An airplane almost always without an engine, a glider, with its small, narrow body and long graceful wings, is towed into the sky by a powered airplane. Once the proper altitude is reached, the towline is released, and the glider soars on its own on warm air currents called thermals.

Although you might think a glider's flight would be fairly short since it has no engine, the opposite is true, with gliders soaring for hundreds of miles. The Soaring Society of America reports that 1,869 miles is the longest glider flight on record. The longest round trip, where the glider started from and returned to the same point, is 1,395 miles.

The sport of soaring is considered both relaxing and challenging and is popular worldwide. Some flight instructors advise students to learn to soar before they begin powered flight instruction, because gliders help them better understand the principles of flight and how to handle aircraft. Almost every major city in the country has a soaring club or glider port where members can learn to soar.

CHAPTER 4

Triumph and Tragedy

When project Mercury came along some of us were skeptical. We had wings on our vehicles and the pilot was in complete control—which we thought was a better approach to space flight.

Armstrong watched with detached interest in 1959 when NASA paraded the seven astronauts of Project Mercury before a public that was hungry for some kind of Cold War victory. Project Mercury, which began in 1958, was the first installment of America's space program and involved its first effort to launch humans into space. It would be followed by projects Gemini and Apollo. The objectives of Project Mercury, which made six manned flights from 1961 to 1963, were:

- To orbit a manned spacecraft around Earth.
- To investigate man's ability to function in space.
- To return both man and spacecraft safely back to Earth.

By 1963, all of the goals for Project Mercury had been successfully met.

The Mercury Seven

The seven military pilots who had survived NASA's grueling test process to become the world's first astronauts (known as "the Mercury Seven") were Alan Shepard, Donald "Deke" Slayton, Wally Schirra, Gordon Cooper, Gus Grissom, Scott Carpenter, and John Glenn.

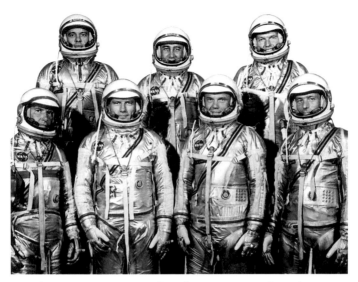

The Mercury Seven pose in their silver space suits. Back row, from the left: Alan Shepard, Gus Grissom, and Gordon Cooper. Front row, from the left: Wally Schirra, Deke Slayton, John Glenn, and Scott Carpenter.

America fell in love with the Mercury Seven. On the surface—thanks to nonstop coverage by *Life* magazine—they were shining examples of the perfect American man, the kind of man that other men wanted to be, and that women wanted to marry. Most of them had combat experience, during either World War II or Korea. They each had thousands of hours flying high-performance aircraft. They were all highly regarded engineers.

The Mercury Seven astronauts instantly became national celebrities, but that wasn't necessarily a good thing. Like Armstrong, these seven professional pilots were focused on their work and their families. They weren't necessarily prepared for constant intrusions by the press. They couldn't understand why people wanted to know what they ate for breakfast, where they prayed, whether they were Boy Scouts, and who their childhood heroes were.

The glare of publicity surrounding the new astronauts was disconcerting to some, but not to John Glenn. Even before he was named as one of the Mercury Seven, Glenn appeared on the TV game show *Name That Tune* alongside ten-year-old Eddie Hodges.

Privacy-loving Neil Armstrong must have cringed as he watched NASA's Mercury Seven jump through hoop after hoop of publicity and public appearances. In fact, he expressed a definite disinterest in becoming an astronaut. While the publicity circus certainly played a role in that, his fundamental reasoning had more to do with why he had become a pilot to begin with.

Project Mercury created a great national debate among test pilots, many of whom scoffed at the idea of being launched into space in a glorified tin can. NASA's original vision for the program called for astronauts to be more like cargo than active participants in the flight. In early renditions, the astronauts were along for the ride but never in total control of the spacecraft. In reality, the space pilots would play a much larger role in the success of each mission than anyone, except the astronauts themselves, had imagined. In the beginning, however, they were the butt of many jokes from those who believed that NASA wasn't looking for skilled pilots, but simply willing passengers.

Neil initially shared that belief, commenting in later years that "when project Mercury came along some of us were skeptical. We had wings on our vehicles and the pilot was in complete control—which we thought was a better approach to space flight."

The First Astronauts

"Astro-chimp" Ham is welcomed home after his flight into space aboard a Mercury Redstone rocket.

The first "astronauts" of Project Mercury were *not* the seven men introduced to the public in 1958, but a series of chimpanzees who were strapped into space capsules and launched skyward so that NASA could test the impact of space flight on the primates. Chimps named Able, Baker, Ham, and Enos all endured various levels of stress and discomfort (in exchange for banana pellets) to pave the way for human space exploration. This only added fuel to the arguments of those who didn't feel astronauts were true pilots but simply passengers with no more control than "Spam in a can."

However, each of the Mercury launches encountered its own series of problems and challenges that often required manual flight; in every case, the launch would have failed miserably if not for the skill and knowledge of the men sitting inside the spacecraft. Project Mercury proved not only that men could survive in space, but that they could triumph there as well.

So Armstrong watched the early stages of Project Mercury from a safe distance, turning his immediate attention toward a new flight challenge and a new member of the family, baby Karen Anne, nicknamed Muffie, who was born in 1959.

The X-15 Program

Although Neil had dismissed the idea of being an astronaut, his next flight test assignment would take him well into the farthest reaches of the atmosphere. As a pilot of the X-15

Neil Armstrong climbs into the cockpit of the X-15 rocket plane; he would climb to heights exceeding two hundred thousand feet and fly at speeds in excess of four thousand miles an hour.

experimental **rocket plane**, Neil would tickle the edge of space, climbing to an altitude of more than two hundred thousand feet at speeds in excess of four thousand miles an hour. The X-15 program began in June 1959 with initial flights made by Scott Crossfield, who would gain the title "fastest man on Earth" by shattering Mach 2 (two times the speed of sound).

Born of a desire to press the limits and the potential of hypersonic flight (flying more than five times the speed of sound), the X-15 program was arguably the most successful flight test project ever. Indeed, several of its test pilots would actually earn their astronaut wings by taking the sturdy aircraft more than fifty miles above Earth and into what NASA considered legitimate "space." According to most scientists, "outer space" actually begins at 62.5 miles above Earth's surface.

Although the test pilots of the X-15 rocket plane and the "newfangled" astronauts of Project Mercury had a professional rivalry, the two programs paralleled each other in many ways. Both helped to solve problems and settle questions about space

The X-15 is carried to an altitude of forty-five thousand feet strapped under the wing of a massive B-52 bomber.

flight. Mercury focused on man's ability to survive and function in space, while the X-15 demonstrated man's ability to control a high-performance aircraft in a "near-space environment." The X-15 program attained its goals of flying faster than Mach 6 and higher than thirty-eight miles.

The X-15 program was a perfect complement to Neil Armstrong's methodical yet adventurous nature. A huge B-52 bomber would carry the much smaller X-15 under its wing to an altitude of forty-five thousand feet. There it would release pilot and aircraft into the thinning air. Inside the X-15, Armstrong would begin the procedures to fire the rocket engine and shoot toward the blackness of space. On one occasion, however, he initiated the firing sequence only to be met by silence, and the X-15 began to drop toward Earth. Neil forced himself to carefully repeat all the steps necessary to ignite the engine. This time he was successful, and the X-15 reversed its fall and rocketed spaceward.

It was by no means the only example of Neil Armstrong's ability to remain calm under extreme pressure.

Working as an Engineer

As Armstrong worked with the X-15 program, the engineer side of his personality began to dominate. He became heavily involved in designing an adaptive control system for the experimental aircraft. Prior to Armstrong's involvement, the hand movements necessary to steer the rocket plane changed as it gained speed. Pilots could easily oversteer the aircraft when it was moving quickly. Armstrong wanted to perfect a self-adjusting system so that a pilot could expect the same response from any given hand motion at any given speed. In other words, a pilot should not have to steer with his whole hand at lower speeds but only with his fingertips at high **velocity**; he should be able to steer the same way at any speed.

At the same time, Armstrong became involved with another space-oriented initiative known as the Dyna-Soar Project. The Dyna-Soar program, also known as the X-20, was initiated by the U.S. Air Force and is considered an early version of the space shuttle. The air force wanted to send a single-man, winged, reusable vehicle into space.

An artist's rendering of the X-20 Dyna-Soar. With its reusable design, it was the precursor to today's space shuttle.

The Space Shuttle

NASA's official name for the shuttle is STS or Space Transportation System. The STS is currently used for human space flight and carries astronauts and payloads into low Earth orbit (considered anywhere from 124 to 1,240 miles above the planet's surface). A payload is something other than a human being that is carried by the shuttle, such as parts for the space station, a satellite to be launched, or various experiments to be performed.

The first space shuttle was launched on April 12, 1981. Like the ill-fated Dyna-Soar, the shuttle was designed to be reused. Five STS orbiters were built. Three remain in service: the *Atlantis*, the *Discovery*, and the *Endeavour*. The other two—the *Challenger* and the *Columbia*—both suffered catastrophic explosions, killing the crew and destroying the spacecraft. *Challenger* exploded upon launch in 1986; *Columbia*, during reentry in 2003. Despite advancements in science and technology, space travel continues to be dangerous. NASA plans to retire the aging shuttle fleet in 2010 and replace it with the *Orion*, a new spacecraft capable of taking humans to the moon and beyond.

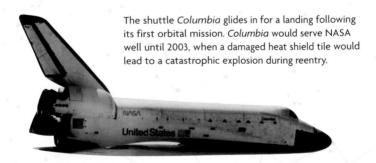

The shuttle *Columbia* glides in for a landing following its first orbital mission. *Columbia* would serve NASA well until 2003, when a damaged heat shield tile would lead to a catastrophic explosion during reentry.

It was a good idea that was ahead of its time and plagued by numerous stumbling blocks, not the least of which was its competition with NASA's efforts. But for Armstrong and many other test pilots, the X-20 was what a spaceship should be. Pilots, they reasoned, should fly in aircraft with wings, not in "capsules"—as the Mercury spacecraft had been dubbed, much to the disapproval of the astronauts.

For a guy who didn't want to be an astronaut, all of Armstrong's efforts in the late 1950s and early 1960s seemed to be leading him into space!

A Family Tragedy

In 1961, the unthinkable happened. While on a family trip to Seattle, Washington, little Muffie tripped and bumped her head, causing a nosebleed and a small bump. The family didn't think much of the incident until they noticed she seemed to be having trouble with her vision. Concerned that she might have a concussion, Neil and Jan took her to a local doctor, who pronounced her fit, but suggested they take her to their family doctor once they got home again. They did so, only to be greeted with the tragic news that she had an inoperable brain tumor.

Muffie's health quickly deteriorated as the tumor began impacting her balance, vision, and motor skills. Radiation treatments gave the Armstrongs a glimmer of hope; the little girl enjoyed a brief remission during which she learned to walk again and began to regain the vigor of a typical two-year-old. But in late 1961, her symptoms returned and she began a downhill slide that ended with her death on January 28, 1962—Neil and Jan's wedding anniversary.

CHAPTER 5

Up in the Air

Why don't you just fix your little problems and light this candle?
    —*Astronaut Al Shepard*

The early 1960s were a dynamic and exciting time in American technology, especially flight and space technology. As Armstrong threw himself into his test-piloting work following the death of his daughter, the Mercury Seven astronauts were making demands regarding their pending spaceflights. The astronauts told NASA that they did not intend to be "Spam in a can," as test pilot Chuck Yeager had reportedly called them. They wanted control of the spacecraft—they wanted to actually fly it. As a result, the program began to change from launches, where the astronaut was present but the flight was mainly controlled from the ground, to the active participation of skilled professional pilots.

The Space Race Heats Up

On April 12, 1961, America got a shock much bigger than the one delivered by Sputnik. This time the Russians announced that they had

Russian cosmonaut Yuri Gagarin becomes the first man in space on April 12, 1961. Up to that point, America had only managed to launch a few monkeys.

achieved yet another first: A Soviet cosmonaut named Yuri Gagarin had become the first human being to fly in space. Aboard his spacecraft, *Vostok 1*, Gagarin had orbited Earth one time.

American scientists were caught off guard. Most people assumed that Sputnik had been a fluke. Most people assumed that America had far more technological skill than the Soviet Union. Suddenly it became very clear that the USSR was a serious contender in the space race. America could not afford to be casual, but it was not yet ready to send a man into orbit. The best NASA could offer was to attempt to launch a man into space for a brief visit. He would not circle Earth as Gagarin had done, but at least he would get a taste of weightlessness and the challenges of space travel. Something had to be done. Russia was clearly gaining the lead. The world now turned its attention toward the United States to see how it would respond.

The response was Alan Shepard. On May 5, 1961, NASA launched Shepard and his *Freedom 7* Mercury capsule into the sky for a fifteen-minute suborbital hop. It wasn't as impressive as Gagarin's actual orbit of Earth, but it showed that America was not going to sit back and let Russia claim the heavens.

The United States responded to Yuri Gagarin's flight by quickly launching Alan Shepard, pictured here, aboard a Mercury Redstone rocket for a brief suborbital hop on May 5, 1961.

Shortly after Shepard, Gus Grissom made a slightly longer suborbital launch in the *Liberty Bell 7* Mercury spacecraft. Once again, it was a successful flight, except that Gus's capsule hatch blew shortly after splashdown, causing the spacecraft to sink and prompting a hasty helicopter rescue of one soggy, frustrated astronaut.

NASA's New Challenges

The first two Mercury flights were enough to give America hope that NASA could effectively respond to the Russian challenge. They also were encouraging to Neil Armstrong, who continued to monitor the space race and consider the role he might play in conquering these new frontiers.

Although Armstrong still preferred the idea of winged aircraft, even for space travel, his interest was piqued with John Glenn's orbital flight on February 20, 1962. For almost an hour and a half, Glenn and his *Friendship 7* spacecraft circled Earth at 17,544 miles per hour, achieving three full orbits (two more than the Russians!) before splashing down southeast of Bermuda.

America's space program had finally come of age, and there was no turning back. NASA now began eyeing the challenges of extended space flight. After all, a flight to the moon would

John Glenn—shown in *Friendship 7*— was the first American to actually orbit Earth. The spacecraft made three full orbits on February 20, 1962.

The Explosive Hatch

Gus Grissom's Mercury spacecraft was equipped with a special explosive hatch that allowed the astronaut to exit the machine quickly in the event of an emergency. The hatch could also be triggered from the outside, in case the astronaut was unconscious or unable to detonate it.

Liberty Bell 7 had seventy bolts on the hatch that were linked to a detonating device buried in the seal around the door. Upon splashdown, Grissom's job was to remove the pin, press a plunger, and blow the door. Something went wrong, however, and the hatch blew off long before Gus was ready. He had to climb out of the sinking spacecraft and tread water until help arrived. He was fished out of the Atlantic as the sea poured into his already heavy space suit.

NASA decided it needed a much more secure door on its spacecraft. Engineers set out to make certain there were no repeat performances of the *Liberty Bell 7* debacle. Sadly for Gus, they would not succeed. Securing the hatch would later claim Grissom's life as he prepared for the launch of *Apollo 1* in 1967.

Astronaut Gus Grissom is hauled to safety after splashdown of *Liberty Bell 7*, when the hatch detonated and the capsule filled with water.

take many days. Now that it was known that humans could survive in space, NASA needed to figure out how long they could survive—and how well. Many other details of manned space flight also needed to be resolved: How does a man eat in space? How does he go to the bathroom? Can he survive and function outside the spacecraft (in a space suit, of course, because there is no air to breathe in space)? All these questions had to be answered if America hoped to send men into space for longer than an hour or two.

Becoming an Astronaut Candidate

To answer these questions, NASA would need many more of the adventurous, highly skilled "throttle jockeys" known as astronauts. On April 18, 1962, NASA announced that it was accepting applications for a new group of astronauts. Among the 253 pilots who submitted their names for consideration was one Neil Alden Armstrong.

The requirements for the new astronauts fit Armstrong to a T. NASA wanted college graduates, six feet tall or less, with degrees in science or engineering. The new candidates needed to be experienced jet test pilots with many hours in high-performance aircraft. Armstrong was all of the above.

Neil Armstrong continued to work in the X-15 program even as he prepared for a battery of astronaut tests at Brooks Air Force Base in San Antonio, Texas. Although the new candidates weren't put through as much agony and embarrassment as the Mercury astronauts, they still had to jump through their share of mysterious hoops.

Many years later, Armstrong recalled that one of the more unpleasant tests included having ice water pumped into his ear for a long period of time. During another test, Armstrong was placed in a black room with no sound, no smell, and no light. He was supposed to remain there for two hours, during which time he sat in a corner and sang to himself until he had estimated his time was up. Yet another test placed Armstrong in a room that could get as hot as 145 degrees Fahrenheit. Considering that Armstrong had flown at Edwards Air Force Base in temperatures well in excess of a hundred degrees, this particular test was probably less stressful for him than for those stationed in chillier climates.

None of the astronaut candidates was completely sure why some of the tests were conducted. Neil later noted that "my sense at the time was that some of these things must have been specifically designed to be medical research rather than diagnostic techniques." In other words, he suspected that perhaps the doctors and scientists weren't just testing the astronaut candidates to see how their bodies would hold up in space, but also using them as human guinea pigs to perform medical experiments.

The requirements for the new astronauts fit Armstrong to a T.

Armstrong easily made it onto the short list of astronaut candidates. Out of thirty-two finalists, he was one of only two civilian pilots, the other being Elliott See Jr. of Texas.

As if being an astronaut finalist wasn't enough, Armstrong was given another honor in 1962 when he received the Octave Chanute Award from the Institute of Aerospace Sciences. The award came as a result of his design work on the adaptive control system for the X-15. But Neil's involvement in the X-15 research, as well as his participation in the failing Dyna-Soar program, would soon come to a screeching halt as he started a new phase of his life. This phase would allow him to truly leave his mark not only on this world, but on one beyond it.

CHAPTER 6

Astronaut!

Our son became an astronaut today.
        —Viola Armstrong

NASA had many ways to inform the public of new astronaut selections. The national media, especially in the Mercury days, flocked to the quiet towns of Cocoa Beach and Cape Canaveral, Florida, for pictures, interviews, and inspirational glimpses of astronauts and astronaut wannabes. Cape Canaveral was the actual site of the launches, but the astronauts hung out in nearby Cocoa Beach. The media responded to America's fascination with astronauts by writing story after story about these "steely-eyed missile men." But Neil Armstrong may have been the only astronaut candidate to have his selection announced on a game show!

The TV show *I've Got a Secret* ran for many years on CBS and entertained viewers by featuring guests who had "a secret." A panel of celebrities then had to ask questions

Garry Moore, host of the television show *I've Got a Secret,* introduced America to the parents of brand-new astronaut Neil Armstrong on September 17, 1962.

of the guest and try to figure out the secret. On the night of September 17, 1962, America was introduced to Stephen and Viola Armstrong, who seated themselves to the right of host Garry Moore and whispered their secret to him: "Our son became an astronaut today."

After several rounds of questions, actress Betsy Palmer was able to guess the Armstrongs' secret, thus depriving them of the show's top prize—eighty dollars to anyone who could stump the panel.

Neil Armstrong had no idea that his parents were appearing on the show. NASA was keeping its new astronauts busy and under wraps. But Armstrong had already received the coveted phone call from Deke Slayton, who now headed the Astronaut Office and made the life-changing decisions about who flew and when. Never one to waste words, Deke's invitation had been short and sweet: "Are you still interested in the astronaut group?"

Despite his earlier misgivings about the space program, Armstrong did not hesitate this time. "Yes, Sir!"

Becoming an Astronaut

In mid-September 1962, Neil was formally introduced to America as one of "the New Nine," as the second astronaut group was dubbed. Also making the cut were air force major Frank Borman, navy lieutenant Charles "Pete" Conrad, navy lieutenant commander James Lovell Jr., air force captain James McDivitt, civilian Elliott See Jr., air force captain Thomas Stafford, air force captain Edward White III, and navy lieutenant commander John Young.

Although America worshipped the astronauts as if they were rock stars or movie idols, their day-to-day work was anything but glamorous. The New Nine immediately went back

Deke Slayton (1924–1993)

Deke Slayton was slated to become the fourth American in space, but his medical tests showed an irregular heartbeat. Although the condition had never caused any problems during his days as a combat and test pilot, NASA did not want to risk the bad publicity of a medical crisis in space. Slayton was pulled from the Mercury program.

Frustrated but determined to regain his spot in the rotation, Deke took control of the newly formed Astronaut Office at Johnson Space Center in Houston, Texas. There he became one of the most powerful men in the early space program, overseeing astronaut activities and training, deciding who flew and when, and generally protecting "his guys" from the distractions of the outside world.

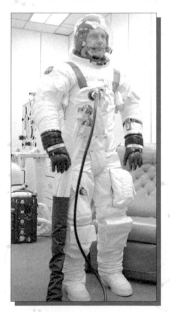

By 1972, Slayton succeeded in his crusade to return to active status and was chosen as docking module pilot in the joint Apollo-Soyuz Test Project (ASTP) mission with Russia. When President Ford interviewed the Apollo crew, he asked Slayton what advice he had for young people. Without hesitation the "world's oldest rookie"—who had waited seventeen years for his space flight—said, "Decide what you want to do . . . and never give up till you've done it."

After years of sending other men into space, Deke Slayton finally suits up for the Apollo-Soyuz Test Project in 1975.

The New Nine astronauts were introduced to the public in late 1962. Pictured from the left, back row, are Elliott See, James McDivitt, James Lovell, Edward White, and Thomas Stafford; front row, Charles Conrad, Frank Borman, Neil Armstrong, and John Young.

to school so that they were fully prepared for their upcoming spaceflights. Time was something they had little of as they rushed from hands-on training to survival school, classroom studies on topics such as orbital mechanics, publicity appearances, and continuing proficiency training in jet aircraft such as the T-33, T-38, and F-102.

They "enjoyed" periodic flights in an aircraft endearingly dubbed "the vomit comet." This was a Boeing KC-135 that could create periods of weightlessness by climbing steeply into the air then dropping into a sharp dive that simulated **zero gravity** for a few seconds. The experience gave astronaut trainees the opportunity to see how their bodies would react to weightlessness.

Deke Slayton assigned each of the new astronauts a special area that would become his area of expertise. This might be a part of the spacecraft, or it might be an aspect of the mission. One astronaut was assigned cockpit layout; another got electrical systems; still another, recovery and reentry. Neil Armstrong was

Riding the Vomit Comet

The episodes of weightlessness created by the Boeing KC-135 were known as parabolas—a term borrowed from geometry to describe a shape that looks like a roller-coaster hill. Although weightlessness is often called *zero gravity*, this is not an accurate term. And, in fact, neither is *weightlessness*. You do not lose your weight—nor does gravity go away. During a parabola, you are in a state of free fall in which you briefly lose your sense of being pulled toward the ground. The feeling of weightlessness occurs because you and the airplane are falling at the same speed and the airplane cannot exert pressure on you. Since there are no objects pushing or pulling on your body, you feel as though you're floating. So in this state of free fall, astronauts were able to float around the cabin for about fifteen seconds, offering them an opportunity to tumble through the air, bounce off the walls, and, more often than not, throw up . . . literally, *up*.

Astronauts test the world of weightlessness inside the "vomit comet," an aircraft flying a zero-gravity trajectory.

handed the responsibility for trainers and simulators. A simulator is a grounded machine designed to give a pilot or an astronaut the feeling of actually flying a specific aircraft or spacecraft. In a *Life* magazine article, Armstrong emphasized the importance of simulators for training purposes. "We can't afford to wait until we're in trouble on an actual flight before we start figuring out ways to solve it."

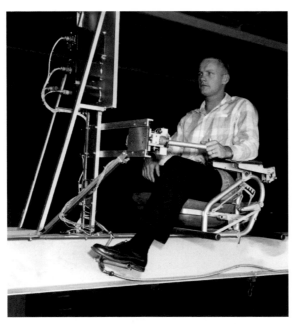

As a research pilot, Neil Armstrong operates the Iron Cross Attitude Simulator in preparation for flying the X-15.

Living in the Spotlight

The Ohio native quickly fell into the astronaut pace. It was a hectic lifestyle, but Armstrong was used to the stress and intensity of being a test pilot. The astronaut business was similar, except for the blinding glare of the media spotlight. Few of the original astronauts—or those who followed them in the program—were comfortable being pegged as celebrities.

Simulators

The first well-known flight simulators were produced by Edwin Link and were known as Link Trainers. In the beginning, they weren't much more than metal boxes perched atop a pump that moved the box up and down. The student would climb into the trainer and close the lid. There he would operate a stick and rudder much like in a real airplane. An electrical suction pump would respond to his stick movements and make the box pitch, yaw, or roll, similar to an aircraft.

As aviation and space research advanced, simulators grew more realistic. Many of the early computer-generated simulations have evolved into computer games. Today's computer flight simulators are far more advanced than the real simulators used in the Apollo space program. And today's NASA and military flight simulators can duplicate dusk, night, daylight, fog, and almost any other atmospheric condition. When you're seated in a modern simulator, it's almost impossible to tell that you aren't flying the real thing.

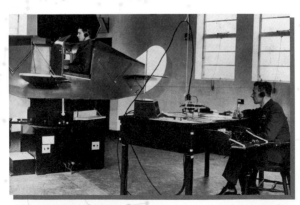

The Link Trainer was an early simulator that helped pilots learn how to maneuver an airplane. In this photo, a Royal Air Force pilot (left) receives flight instruction (from man seated on right) while inside a Link Trainer.

Most had been trained as combat pilots and engineers. Their comfort zone was among their buddies and in situations they could control with their brains or their guts. None of them knew quite how to manage the media or the adoring fans who flocked to Cocoa Beach, Florida, and Houston, Texas, hoping to get a glimpse of one of the famous fly boys.

Armstrong dealt with fame as he dealt with everything else—quietly and methodically. His fellow astronauts regarded him as someone who didn't quite fit the outgoing-pilot mold. Yet they all respected him and acknowledged that he knew how to keep his cool in any situation. Astronaut Dave Scott noted that Armstrong was never frantic, never distracted by problems. Instead, he reacted with speed and accuracy. "He could make an analysis of a problem very quickly. The guy was really cool under pressure," Scott noted. Armstrong would need those qualities in the coming months and years.

. . . he knew how to keep his cool in any situation.

An Almost Fatal Fire

By 1964, the Armstrong family was settled in El Lago, Texas. Baby Mark had joined the family in April 1963, and Ricky was a thriving six-year-old. Jan had become friends with the other astronauts' wives. Neil was working long hours developing simulators that could help the astronauts prepare for real space flight.

Then suddenly the family found itself once again face-to-face with near tragedy. On April 24, 1964, Jan woke Neil at 3:45 a.m. to tell him the house was rapidly filling with smoke. Neil went to investigate and yelled to Jan that the house was on fire; they needed to call the fire department and get out.

Unable to reach emergency services by phone, Jan frantically sought the help of neighbors Ed and Pat White. While Pat summoned the fire department, Ed—himself an astronaut—grabbed a hose and headed into the Armstrongs' backyard. Meanwhile, Neil carried baby Mark down the hall through the acrid haze, calling for Jan to come grab the baby. By the time he went back for Ricky, the smoke had turned thick, black, and toxic. He could no longer simply hold his breath; he had to throw a wet towel over his head and bend below the heat and fumes. Neil

An Armstrong family portrait from 1969: Neil; Jan; Ricky, age twelve; and Mark, age six.

pushed into Ricky's room and grabbed the six-year-old, throwing the wet towel over his son's head. Once Ricky was secure in the backyard, Neil and Ed began moving cars and other belongings that could be safely separated from the burning home.

Luckily, because of a broken air conditioner, the family had been sleeping with their windows open, which provided enough fresh air to counteract the smoke long enough for Neil to retrieve the youngsters and rush them to safety.

Despite the horror of the night, the entire family emerged unharmed. Even Super, the family dog who had been Ricky's constant companion since his sister's death, had managed to escape the flames. It was later determined that faulty wiring had started the blaze.

CHAPTER 7

Project Gemini Begins

Eight days in a garbage can.

—Pete Conrad's description of his Gemini Flight

As the Mercury program wound down, Project Gemini fell into place. Its goals were more complex than the Mercury program and included:

- To subject humans and equipment to spaceflight up to two weeks in duration.
- To rendezvous, dock, and maneuver with orbiting vehicles.
- To perfect reentering the atmosphere and landing at a specific point on land.

Gemini was named for the astrological sign of the Twins, because it would feature a two-man spacecraft. Unlike the Mercury flights, which basically tested how spaceflight impacted people physically and mentally,

Project Gemini, named for the astrological Twins, appropriately featured two astronauts on each flight. In this photo, Wally Schirra and Tom Stafford prepare for their *Gemini VI* flight, during which they would rendezvous with *Gemini VII*, carrying Frank Borman and Jim Lovell.

Gemini was designed to figure just how much could be accomplished in space. Could astronauts survive for long periods of time—weeks, not days? Could two ships rendezvous with each other and actually dock together in space? Could the astronauts step outside and work in the vacuum of space? Gemini was poised to answer these questions and many more. There was now plenty of work to do—and Neil Armstrong was in the thick of it!

Playing Backup

As the Armstrongs rebuilt their home and settled back into a daily routine, Neil got word that he had been named to the backup crew of *Gemini V*. Being assigned as backup meant that he would be training right alongside the prime crew. Armstrong was tapped as backup commander, while his friend Elliott See trained as backup pilot. They would be standbys for two of the more colorful characters in the astronaut corps, Gordon Cooper and Pete Conrad.

Pete and "Gordo" were a lively, fun-loving duo. In fact, NASA was a little uneasy about sending Gordo back into space. The slow-talking Oklahoma boy was a highly skilled pilot, but he tended to push the limits of what NASA considered acceptable astronaut behavior. Pete Conrad, too, had been known to thumb his nose at authority, but he had considerably more discipline than Gordo.

Both Cooper and Conrad had personalities that were in sharp contrast with Armstrong and See, who were more typical of the focused, quiet engineer type. Surprisingly, the two sets of polar opposites hit it off quite well. Armstrong was comfortable working with Gordo and was confident that anything Cooper missed would be caught by the hard-charging Conrad.

Gordon Cooper (1927–2004)
Pushing the Limits

Gordon Cooper was a highly skilled pilot but also a bit of a show off. He tested—and sometimes exceeded—the limits of NASA's patience.

Gordon Cooper loved to bedevil NASA officials by violating rules of common sense when it came to aircraft operation. Shortly before his 1963 *Faith 7* flight, the Mercury astronaut almost lost his active status when he decided to buzz Mercury operations manager Walt Williams in an F-102. Williams leapt to his feet in the second-story office as Cooper hit the afterburners on his jet. The NASA manager was horrified to look outside and see Cooper's jet streak by beneath the window!

Because of his prank, Gordo barely kept his Mercury flight; even then, it was only thanks to Deke Slayton's smooth-talking assurances to Williams. Slayton promised to keep a tight rein on Gordo until the launch date. But it was Cooper who had the last laugh. When his *Faith 7* Mercury flight experienced a catastrophic loss of most of its systems, Cooper used his superb test-piloting skills to manually fly the craft safely back to Earth against overwhelming odds. It was a triumph of man over machinery, and even Walt Williams had to grudgingly admit, "Gordo, you were the right man for the mission."

At the same time that Armstrong was backing up *Gemini V*, he was doing support work for Gus Grissom and John Young, who were preparing to launch in *Gemini III*, which Commander Grissom had wryly named the *Molly Brown*. Recalling the disaster of losing the *Liberty Bell 7* beneath the waves of the Atlantic, Grissom decided it might be good luck to name his Gemini spacecraft for a socialite who had survived the sinking of the *Titanic* and was dubbed "the Unsinkable Molly Brown."

Although NASA officials frowned upon Grissom's choice of name, it was most accurate. The *Molly Brown* delivered a flawless flight (and, yes, she *did* prove to be unsinkable!). The only real squabble came after splashdown when Grissom's pilot, John Young, admitted that he had smuggled a corned beef sandwich into space. Mercury astronaut Wally Schirra—a tireless joker—had delivered the sandwich to Young the night before the launch. Up to that point, space food was pretty unpleasant. Astronauts had to eat freeze-dried packs of food that resembled Styrofoam, or tubes of gel that could be squeezed directly into their mouths.

Because of zero gravity, something like a corned beef sandwich would quickly separate and begin floating about the cabin. NASA was understandably concerned about fouling the delicate instruments with stray strands of sauerkraut or wayward globs of Thousand Island dressing. Fortunately Young and Grissom had the good sense to keep their corned beef sandwich under wraps through most of the flight.

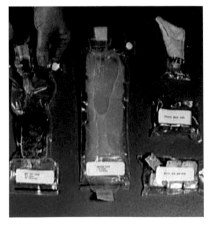

Early space food looked and tasted more like sawdust than it did real food.

Despite the occasional unintentional (or intentional) astronaut-induced challenges, the Gemini program was achieving all its goals with considerable efficiency—despite some electrical problems that forced the cancellation of several planned projects. Still, Cooper and Conrad proved that humans *could* function in space long enough to travel to the moon. They spent eight days in the spacecraft with no long-term ill effects, although Conrad later described it as "eight days in a garbage can." They also tested the spacecraft's navigation and guidance system, paving the way for future Gemini to rendezvous and dock. *Rendezvous* meant moving the spacecraft close to each other, while *docking* meant that they actually connected and flew through space as one unit.

Extra-Vehicular Activity (EVA)

Gemini VI and *VII* perfected the rendezvous technique, and now it was up to *Gemini VIII* to nail the docking. Armstrong was very pleased when Deke Slayton assigned him to command the *Gemini VIII* mission. His *Gemini V* backup pilot, Elliott See, was given command of *Gemini IX*, and Armstrong was assigned a new partner for his first mission, Dave Scott, who had just joined NASA with a third group of astronauts.

Dave Scott and Neil Armstrong, pictured here in *Gemini VIII* flight, rendezvoused and docked with the Agena target vehicle.

In addition to the docking challenge, *Gemini VIII's* objectives called for an EVA, which stood for "extra-vehicular activity" and meant that the astronaut would move about *outside* the spacecraft, tethered to a lifeline.

The First EVA

The first EVA, completed by Ed White during the *Gemini IV* mission, had been both awe inspiring and near disastrous. Despite being one of the most athletic men in the astronaut corps, Ed had a great deal of trouble maneuvering outside the spacecraft. His visor became fogged, and he had difficulty getting back into the Gemini capsule. During that time, his heart rate shot up to 180 beats per minute as he struggled for some measure of control.

Inside the spacecraft, Commander Jim McDivitt grimly recalled their EVA training. He knew that according to established procedures, if an astronaut could not manage to get safely back into the spacecraft, the commander must cut him loose and return to Earth alone. It was a scenario no one even wanted to think about. Fortunately, after a physically draining twenty-minute space walk, Ed White managed to struggle back into the cabin and return safely home.

Astronaut Ed White became the first human to complete a successful space walk. This image shows White floating in zero gravity. He is attached to the spacecraft only by the length of gold cord seen here.

A perilous *Gemini IV* space walk had taught NASA that a space walk was anything but a cakewalk. Thus Dave Scott was selected for the *Gemini VIII* EVA not only for his piloting skills and his graduate studies on rendezvous, but also for his strength and athletic skill.

Tragedy in the Sky

If Armstrong's schedule had been hectic before *Gemini VIII* training, it became even more frenetic as he and Scott threw themselves into training for what would be the most complex mission yet.

Then, two weeks before the scheduled March launch, the astronauts found themselves mourning two of their own, including one of Armstrong's best friends.

It was standard operating procedure for astronauts to travel frequently. Because of the potential delays of commercial flight, NASA provided the pilots with T-38 jet trainers that they used to crisscross the country for training, equipment consultations, and speaking engagements.

Elliott See and Charles Bassett of the *Gemini XI* prime crew had been on their way to the McDonnell Aircraft Corporation's facility in St. Louis, Missouri, to log practice time in one of the company's simulators. Bad weather and poor visibility caused See to overshoot the runway. As he banked his aircraft left to try again, the T-38 dropped too low and smashed into the very building where technicians were working on his Gemini spacecraft. Both men were killed instantly.

Gemini astronauts Elliott See (left) and Charlie Bassett lost their lives when their T-38 crashed into a building at the McDonnell aircraft plant in St. Louis. Elliott and Neil had been good friends.

It was just another reminder that the astronauts were simply high-profile test pilots. Neil had learned back at Edwards that death was the only companion a test pilot could be certain of. Elliott See was not the first friend Neil had lost, nor would he be the last.

CHAPTER 8

Into Space

We have serious problems here. We're tumbling end over end. We've disengaged from the Agena.

—Dave Scott

Neil Armstrong dealt with the death of Elliott See as he dealt with all tragedy: by focusing his energy and emotion on his work. With only two weeks to go before the launch of *Gemini VIII*, there was little time to ponder matters of life and death, at least not directly. In reality, of course, everything Armstrong and Scott worked on was a matter of life and death! *Gemini VIII* was going to be the most demanding and complex mission to date. And it was both astronauts' first time in space. It was critical that the duo understood what needed to be done and trusted their own abilities to do it.

Although NASA had eliminated the practice of naming spacecraft, the space agency did permit astronauts to design **mission patches**, a custom that continues today. Armstrong and Scott paid tribute to the program itself by featuring the original Gemini Twins of mythology, Castor and Pollux, on their mission patch.

A color design for the *Gemini VIII* mission patch.

The *Gemini VIII* Mission

In addition to the rendezvous, docking, and the EVA objectives, the *Gemini VIII*

The Agena target vehicle is launched into space on an Atlas rocket in preparation for Neil Armstrong's *Gemini VIII* mission.

mission assignments for Armstrong and Scott included observing frog egg growth to see how embryos reacted to space conditions, conducting nuclear emulsion tests to study fast-charged nuclear particles, and completing a variety of photographic projects. But the truly significant achievement would be a successful docking with the Agena—an unmanned spacecraft that had been launched into orbit for just that purpose.

Docking was critical because, in order to fly to the moon, the astronauts would have to travel there in a command and service module, climb into a **lunar** module—known as the LM and pronounced *lem*—then undock from the command module and head for the moon's surface. If they wanted to get back home again, they would have to fly the LM back to the command module, dock with it, and climb back in. NASA needed to make sure that all the parts and pieces of this huge project had been successfully achieved many times. Only then could astronauts be sent to the moon.

The Gemini Spacecraft

Neil and his Gemini "twin" Dave Scott are strapped into their spacecraft during the pre-launch countdown.

The spacecraft that Neil Armstrong and Dave Scott would pilot on the *Gemini VIII* mission was designed by the McDonnell Aircraft Corporation, an aerospace manufacturer, as a bridge between the relatively simple Mercury capsule and the larger, more complex Apollo spacecraft that would eventually fly a man to the moon. The Gemini program's mission was also more detailed than Mercury's.

Gemini was America's second step toward the moon. NASA needed to know that its astronauts and its machines were prepared for long-duration spaceflights. The Gemini spacecraft, however, was not especially well equipped for *comfortable* long-term flights. There was little legroom, and most of the interior consisted of instrument panels, lights, and gauges. The instruments were very similar to those used in contemporary military aircraft. Early on, the Gemini capsule earned the nickname "the Gusmobile" because astronaut Gus Grissom had been so involved in the spacecraft's overall design and layout. In fact, some of the taller astronauts complained that the capsule was so cramped because Gus had designed it to perfectly fit his five-foot, nine-inch frame.

Launched into Space

On March 16, 1966, Armstrong climbed into the cramped crew compartment of *Gemini VIII* and waited patiently as the NASA launch technicians secured him and Scott into the spacecraft. Although bigger than the Mercury ships, Gemini offered no space for stretching or moving around. One astronaut had likened his Gemini mission to traveling into space in the front seat of a Volkswagen Beetle.

Armstrong's parents were on hand for the launch. They were understandably nervous about watching their son roar into space atop many tons of highly explosive rocket fuel, but the launch went

A portrait in concentration: Neil Armstrong completes final adjustments and instrument checks before the launch of *Gemini VIII*.

smoothly as *Gemini VIII* disappeared into a clear blue Florida sky. After a little over six minutes of flight, the spacecraft began circling Earth—known as orbiting—about ninety-six miles high in space. It was traveling about twelve hundred miles behind the Agena and would use the next four orbits to catch up and prepare for docking.

After only three orbits, Armstrong radioed to Mission Control that he had spotted the Agena. The Gemini spacecraft was now keeping pace with the Agena, as both machines orbited at a rate of 17,295 miles an hour. The mechanics of movement in space are very different from those found on Earth. Armstrong could not just fly up alongside the Agena. In order to overtake the other spacecraft, he actually had to fire his thruster away from it; the Gemini would then drop into a lower orbit, allowing

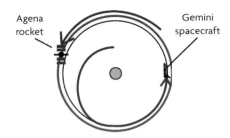

Agena rocket

Gemini spacecraft

This illustration shows how dropping into a lower orbit allows one spacecraft to catch up to another and dock. Being in a lower orbit means that the spacecraft covers more distance faster and, thus, is able to catch up to the target craft (the Agena) and dock.

him to cover more space and catch up. Once he was within sight of the Agena, he would maneuver into the same orbit so that the two ships could dock. Neil later credited his time in simulators with giving him the skills to complete this tricky process.

Rendezvousing with the Agena

With constant updates from Dave Scott, Armstrong began maneuvering the Gemini to its rendezvous station with the Agena. Both men, though seasoned professionals, were excited about their first spaceflight.

"You're 900 feet. Five feet per second," Scott reported, updating Armstrong on how close he was to the Agena and how fast he was moving.

"That's just unbelievable! Unbelievable," Armstrong said, as he positioned the spacecraft near its target. "I can't believe it!"

"Yes, I can't either. Outstanding job, Coach," Scott told his partner.

The duo verbally patted each other on the back and Scott stared at the Agena, which now loomed almost close enough to touch. The two spacecraft were traveling side by side at the same speed, a little over seventeen thousand miles per hour.

"Boy! Look at that sucker! That's beautiful," Dave Scott enthused.

For several hours the Gemini simply kept pace with the Agena—"station keeping," as NASA called it. Then came time for the docking phase.

Docking with the Agena

Armstrong skillfully maneuvered the Gemini's nose cone so it lined up with the Agena's docking mechanism. Moving at a rate of three inches per second, he nudged the Gemini closer and closer to the Agena. In a matter of minutes, the Agena's docking latches clicked and a green light indicated that the docking had been successfully completed.

"Flight, we are docked! Yes, it's really a smoothie," Armstrong radioed back to Mission Control.

NASA had been concerned that the docking process would somehow cause the Agena to roll, but Armstrong reported no such problems: "The Agena was very stable and at the present time we are having no noticeable **oscillations** at all," he radioed.

Down at Mission Control, the staff erupted into cheers and a brief celebration before getting back to business. If the Russians still nursed any dream of beating America to the moon, they would have to kick their efforts into high gear. The Soviet Union had yet to complete a successful rendezvous, let alone docking in space!

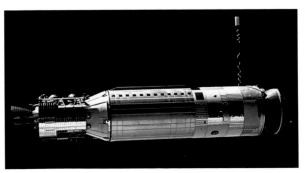

The Agena target vehicle in orbit, about to rendezvous with *Gemini VIII.*

Mission Control Center

Mission Control Center (MCC) in Houston, Texas, became the nerve center for the space program in 1965. There, teams of engineers and technicians monitored spacecraft operation and astronaut well-being for every mission. During the Mercury program, Mission Control was located in Cape Canaveral, Florida (where the launches took place). The move to Houston came mainly because President Lyndon Johnson, a Texan, wanted it so.

As spacecraft evolved, they were built with more systems and **diagnostics** that had once been managed from the ground. Today's Mission Control follows flight activities, helps the crew prepare for maneuvers, and stands by to jump in with guidance in the event of an emergency. In the early days, Mission Control teams were mere youngsters in their twenties, which was probably an advantage since they believed they could do anything—and proved it!

No spaceflight underscored the critical link between astronauts and Mission Control better than the near-tragic *Apollo 13* flight, which began with Commander Jim Lovell's now immortal (if misquoted) words "Okay, Houston, we've had a problem here . . ." The teamwork between Mission Control and the astronauts trapped in a damaged spacecraft made the difference between life and death, earning *Apollo 13* the dubious status of a "successful failure."

The Mission Operations Control Room in Mission Control at Houston's Manned Space Center during the *Apollo 13* mission.

After a few more instructions from Mission Control, Armstrong and Scott prepared for a twenty-one-minute LOS (loss of signal) as the Gemini craft orbited high above the Indian Ocean, temporarily out of reach of the worldwide tracking network. It was after the LOS that NASA got its first indication that something had gone terribly wrong.

A Problem in Space

The previously giddy tone in Dave Scott's voice was noticeably absent when he radioed, "We have serious problems here. We're tumbling end over end. We've disengaged from the Agena . . ."

Prior to delivering that unsettling message, Scott had noticed that the Gemini was no longer in level flight, but was rolling into a thirty-degree bank, as if someone were tilting the spacecraft. Armstrong calmly attempted to adjust the angle, with no success; the tumbling continued. Unable to secure any input from Mission Control due to the LOS, Armstrong made the decision to undock from the Agena, hoping that this was the cause of the problem.

"We have serious problems here. We're tumbling end over end . . ."

Free of the Agena, the small Gemini capsule continued its end-over-end tumble. As the violent revolutions increased beyond 360 degrees per second, Armstrong's vision began to grow blurry. He knew the problem must be resolved quickly or he and Scott would both pass out.

The astronauts decided that one of the Gemini's thrusters was stuck in its firing position, causing the frantic roll. But with sixteen thrusters and a very limited window of time before losing both vision and consciousness, Armstrong had to counteract the problem by firing a different set of thrusters, those used during reentry.

Fortunately for the two astronauts, Armstrong's gamble paid off and he was able to regain control of the spacecraft. Unfortunately for the mission, NASA rules required that any activation of the Reentry Control System (RCS) must be followed by an immediate return to Earth. Only eleven hours into their mission, Neil Armstrong and Dave Scott were headed home. They weren't at all happy about scrubbing, or discontinuing, the remainder of the mission, but at least they were headed home alive.

Neil Armstrong and Dave Scott greet the navy divers helping to secure the *Gemini VIIII* spacecraft after its emergency return to Earth.

CHAPTER 9

Apollo Begins

Fire in the spacecraft . . . We're burning up! Get us out!
        —Roger Chaffee

Although some in the astronaut corps were quick to judge Armstrong's decision to activate *Gemini VIII*'s RCS, Deke Slayton wasn't one of them—and his opinion was one of the few that mattered. Slayton viewed the near disaster as a test of Mission Control's efficiency and a tribute to the cool heads of the two astronauts who were on the hot seat. He also noted that the docking had been successful, despite its short-lived triumph. Neither Armstrong nor Scott would suffer any long-term damage to his NASA career due to the scrubbed Gemini flight. If anything, Slayton had learned he could trust both of them to think through a problem and make a levelheaded decision.

Neither Armstrong nor Scott would suffer any long-term damage to his NASA career due to the aborted Gemini flight.

Gemini IX, X, XI, and *XII* enjoyed increasing levels of success, despite some new and unusual challenges related to docking and EVA. But by the end of the Gemini program and the start of Project Apollo, NASA officials were convinced that President Kennedy's goal of sending a man to the moon and returning him safely to Earth by the end of the 1960s was well within reach. The goals of the Project Apollo were:

- To establish the technology to meet other national interests in space.
- To achieve superiority in space for the United States.
- To carry out a program of scientific exploration of the moon.
- To develop man's capability to work in the lunar environment.

Spirits were high. Hours were long. The work was demanding and intense for everyone at every level of the space program. From the contractors to the astronauts, everyone seemed to sense the delicate balance among speed, accuracy, and safety. Somehow all three had to be achieved in order to put America on the moon. Mistakes—at least major ones—had to be avoided at all costs. However, given all of Project Apollo's delicate equipment, the sheer volume of human involvement, and the overwhelming sense of urgency, mistakes were bound to happen. The first and biggest one cost NASA dearly.

Disaster on the Ground

The day of "the fire," Armstrong was in Washington, D.C. It was January 27, 1967. He, Jim Lovell, Gordon Cooper, Scott Carpenter, and Dick Gordon were at the White House to sign an international space treaty. Back at Cape Canaveral, astronauts Gus Grissom, Ed White, and Roger Chaffee were testing the *Apollo 1* spacecraft that they would be riding into space on February 21. High atop launchpad 34, Gus, Roger, and Ed were sealed into the Apollo command module for what was called a plugs-out test—a kind of dress rehearsal for the launch, with the spacecraft functioning as though it were about to lift off. The three-man Apollo craft was pressurized with pure oxygen, and the astronauts were suited up and strapped into the command module.

Apollo 1 astronauts Gus Grissom, Ed White, and Roger Chaffee pose in front of launchpad 34, where they would ultimately lose their lives in a freak launchpad fire.

Commander Gus Grissom was still frustrated by ongoing quality issues with the *Apollo 1* model. At one point, in fact, he had made his lack of faith public by hanging a lemon from the spacecraft. Although some of the problems had been fixed, the communications system between Apollo and the ground was, in Deke Slayton's words, "pretty lousy." By the evening of January 27, Gus was completely disgusted with his inability to send or receive clear transmissions. "How can we get to the moon if we can't talk between two buildings," he demanded.

Technicians on the ground struggled to find and resolve the problems. And then it happened . . .

"Fire in the spacecraft," came the garbled announcement from Roger Chaffee.

"We're burning up! Get us out!"

By the time Deke Slayton, who was listening nearby in the blockhouse, could make sense of what he was hearing, more than twenty seconds had passed. In those seconds, the three astronauts had been killed by the toxic fumes, and the hull of the spacecraft had exploded from the intense heat.

It was an unthinkable event—something no one had dreamed of. Every astronaut in the program knew that lives would be lost in the conquest of space; none could have guessed that those losses would first occur on the ground.

Returning from dinner in Washington, Armstrong noticed the blinking message light on his hotel room phone. Like his dinner companions, he was stunned by the news. He called home to talk to Jan but got no answer. Jan was sitting uneasily in Pat White's living room. She had received a sketchy call from astronaut Al Bean asking her to head over to Pat's because they heard there had been an accident. Jan had been a test pilot's wife long enough to know that those words would likely be followed by a knock on the door and the worst kind of news.

Astronaut Bill Anders was the grim messenger. The same tragic scene repeated itself in the nearby homes of Betty Grissom and Martha Chaffee. It wasn't that the wives had never braced themselves for bad news; it was just that—like everyone at NASA—they had simply never considered the possibility of disaster striking anywhere but in space.

The *Apollo 1* hatch was a complicated piece of equipment. Under the best of conditions, it took about ninety seconds to get

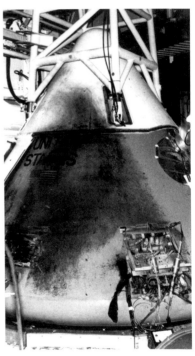

The charred shell of the *Apollo 1* spacecraft one day after a launchpad fire. The tragedy sent NASA back to the drawing board to fix many of the problems associated with the early Apollo program.

the hatch open. It had to be unlatched, and numerous bolts had to be loosened and removed. All this complexity was due, in no small part, to Gus Grissom's unfortunate experience with the loss of the *Liberty Bell 7*. It was an irony that compounded the tragedy of the day's events. Also, just weeks before the fire, Gus Grissom had spoken with a journalist. "We're in a risky business," he'd said, "and we hope if anything happens to us, it will not delay the program. The conquest of space is worth the risk of life."

Armstrong would later describe the post–*Apollo 1* period as "Some very traumatic times. You know, I suppose you're much more likely to accept loss of a friend in flight, bust it really hurt to lose them in a ground test. That was an indictment of ourselves. I mean, [it happened] because we didn't do the right thing somehow. That's doubly, doubly traumatic."

Lessons Learned

The loss of Grissom, White, and Chaffee did, indeed, hit NASA and its contractors like a ton of bricks. Investigations were launched; questions were asked; some people even began arguing to end the space program all together.

Gus Grissom had not been the only person at NASA who was displeased with the Apollo spacecraft and the direction of the whole program. Many had begun to question whether the massive effort would ever really "get off the ground." Literally.

Today there are those who argue that the fire itself, as tragic as it was, served as a much-needed wake-up call. The time spent on the investigation gave everyone a chance to regroup, reflect, and rethink previous strategies and approaches.

"They got time and they fixed a lot of things that needed to be fixed and they never had time to do it before. So we got an added benefit but we regret the price we had to pay," Armstrong recalled.

Investigation of the Fire

Immediately following the *Apollo 1* fire, NASA administrator James Webb convened an internal investigation. Representing the astronaut corps in the investigation was Frank Borman, who oversaw the disassembly of the charred spacecraft. *Apollo 1* was taken apart bolt by bolt, and each piece was thoroughly inspected, photographed, inspected again at a lab, then labeled and placed in a plastic bag in a secure area. After NASA officials had thoroughly reviewed the possible causes, they reported that the combination of a small spark from frayed wiring and a pure oxygen environment had generated a violent blaze. According to the final report, the astronauts did not burn to death but were asphyxiated by carbon monoxide.

During a congressional hearing following the *Apollo 1* fire, NASA astronauts Frank Borman (far left), Jim McDivitt, Deke Slayton, Wally Schirra, and Al Shepard show their support for the space agency and its goals.

The day after the *Apollo 1* investigation report was issued, Deke Slayton called eighteen of the astronauts into his office and announced, "The guys who are going to fly the first lunar missions are the guys in this room."

Neil Armstrong was among them.

CHAPTER 10

Reaching for the Moon

If anything goes wrong here, it's not going to be my fault, because my part is going to be better than I have to make it!

With renewed commitment to excellence and safety, the NASA team threw itself into the Apollo program in the hope of achieving John F. Kennedy's goal: putting a man on the moon by the end of the 1960s. Armstrong's time was consumed by training and by the development of flight simulators.

The Armstrong family was thriving, and Neil tried to devote his weekends to fishing with his sons and time with Jan. The family enjoyed trips to the beach; although Neil and Jan were not big partiers, they especially liked having friends over for dinner.

Armstrong's work was always stressful, but the mood at NASA had lightened considerably, becoming more focused and energetic in the days following the *Apollo 1* fire. From the top of the NASA hierarchy to the least significant contractor, everyone had been rattled by the tragedy.

Armstrong's time was consumed by training and by the development of flight simulators.

Everyone, it seemed, had made a personal commitment to ensure that history did not repeat itself.

Recalling the new mood during a NASA interview in 2001, Armstrong commented, "Every guy in the project, every guy at the bench building something, every assembler, every inspector, every guy that was setting up tests, cranking the torque wrench, is saying, man or woman, 'If anything goes wrong here, it's not going to be my fault, because my part is going to be better than I have to make it!' And when you have hundreds of

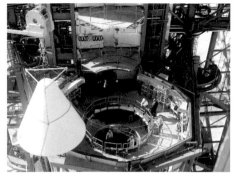

After the *Apollo 1* tragedy, work at NASA continued, as seen in this November 1967 photo of a nose cone being placed onto a new spacecraft.

thousands of people all doing their job a little better than they have to, you get an improvement in performance. And that's the only reason we could have pulled this whole thing off."

In October 1968—almost two years after the launchpad fire— *Apollo 7*, the first manned Apollo mission, was launched. The mission was largely a confidence builder. The spacecraft had been completely redesigned, and NASA wanted the public to know that the program was back on track. Former Mercury astronaut Wally Schirra commanded the eleven-day Apollo mission, accompanied by newcomers Donn Eisele and Walter Cunningham.

Apollo 7 was a success if by no other measure than that it launched, flew, and came home in one piece. Schirra and his crew performed with typical skill and commitment, despite developing head colds in midflight.

The mission patch for *Apollo 7*, featuring the names of the three astronauts who would restore NASA's glory after the tragic *Apollo 1* fire: Wally Schirra, Donn Eisele, and Walt Cunningham.

NASA was now ready to try something spectacular. *Apollo 8* would be just that.

Although the final construction of the LM was taking longer than planned, NASA decided it could still send men to the moon, if only for a sightseeing tour. Simply placing astronauts into the moon's orbit would be a significant achievement.

Saving 1968

The year 1968 was a traumatic one in American history. Students were rioting on college campuses in protest of the war in Southeast Asia, where young Americans were dying on a daily basis. Martin Luther King Jr. was shot and killed. Bobby Kennedy was shot and killed. The North Koreans seized the USS *Pueblo* and accused it of spying. It seemed as though the world had lost its rudder and was spinning wildly out of control. America desperately needed a moment of peace; some small victory to call its own.

On December 21, 1968, Frank Borman, Jim Lovell, and Bill Anders began a six-day journey that no other human being had ever attempted. Their trip into lunar orbit would prove to be a much-needed Christmas present to America.

The 1960s and early 1970s were among the most tumultuous times in American history. Students from Columbia University are pictured here staging a civil rights sit-in and are confronted by counter-demonstrating teachers.

After NASA's two years of regret and retooling and America's year of trauma and social upheaval, there was something uniquely healing about *Apollo 8*'s long-distance broadcast on December 24, 1968. The astronauts each read a passage from the first ten chapters of Genesis while gazing at the brilliant blue planet they called home. The space voyagers signed off with the reassuring words, "Good night, good luck, Merry Christmas . . . and God bless all of you, all of you on the good Earth."

The *Apollo 8* crew (from left to right: Frank Borman, William Anders, and James Lovell) proved that a trip could be made to the moon and back.

It was simple, unscripted, and unrehearsed—and it would become second only to the moon landing in terms of public response. NASA was swamped with letters and telegrams from grateful Americans, one of whom succinctly defined the historic impact of the half-million-mile spaceflight: "You saved 1968."

Armstrong served on the *Apollo 8* backup crew and watched with interest as his colleagues did the impossible. The Apollo spacecraft had only one successful mission under its belt, which was nowhere near the magnitude of a trip to the moon. Likewise,

Earthrise, shot from the *Apollo 8* spacecraft. This remains one of the most stunning photos in human history.

the powerful Saturn V booster—the rocket launcher that would propel the Apollo spacecraft beyond the atmosphere—had only been tested a couple of times and had demonstrated more than its share of problems. Privately, there were those at NASA who questioned the safety and sanity of the mission. Armstrong, however, saw the wisdom of the decision, noting that "the time schedule was becoming an overbearing issue. To get the job done by the end of the decade, we needed to take giant steps and really make lots of progress on each flight, and this was the only way."

The Saturn V Booster

Apollo 9 launches on March 3, 1969. This ten-day Earth-orbit mission is the second test of the Saturn V booster.

To push a spacecraft out of Earth's atmosphere and set it on a course for the moon, NASA needed something big—bigger than any rocket that had ever flown. The Saturn V was a multistage liquid-fuel rocket that remains the most powerful launch vehicle ever used for spaceflight. It consisted of three stages, with each stage containing its own engine and **propellant**.

The first stage pushed the massive spacecraft up to thirty-eight miles high, before separating and falling back to Earth two minutes into flight. The second stage then exploded into action, moving the spacecraft sixty-two miles up to the edge of space. After stage two fell away, stage three pushed the Apollo into its orbit of Earth. Then, later in the flight, it was fired yet again for translunar injection (TLI), which placed the spacecraft on a flight path toward the moon.

The Assignment of a Lifetime

The day before the Genesis transmission, Deke Slayton summoned Armstrong to his office. There he shared the historic news that Neil would command the *Apollo 11* mission—and that, if *Apollo 8* returned safely and all went well on *9* and *10*, Armstrong would likely be captaining the first moon landing.

Although Armstrong had been handed an assignment unlike any in history, he was careful to keep everything in perspective. Many events had to unfold with great precision in order to make *Apollo 11* the moon landing. "A lot of things we just didn't know at that point and I think I did not really expect that we'd get the chance to try a lunar landing on that flight," Neil recalled. "Too many things could go wrong on [*Apollo*] *8*, *9* or *10*, or whatever."

Slayton talked to Armstrong at length about who his crewmates should be. They decided on Edwin "Buzz" Aldrin and Mike Collins.

The prime crew of *Apollo 11:* From the left are astronauts Neil Armstrong, commander; Michael Collins, command module pilot; and Edwin "Buzz" Aldrin Jr., lunar module pilot.

Nineteen sixty-nine began with considerable fanfare and optimism, as President Lyndon Johnson awarded medals to the triumphant crew of *Apollo 8* while NASA made public the names of the *Apollo 11* crew—and the fact that they would be training for a possible lunar landing.

For Neil Armstrong, always the calm and focused engineer, it was business as usual. He and his crewmates threw themselves into training for what would certainly be the longest— and arguably the most significant—flight of the twentieth century.

Flying the LLTV

As pilots and astronauts have learned time and again, even training can be a dangerous proposition. But few aspects of Apollo preparation were as dangerous as flying the awkward, spider-legged device known as the LLTV or Lunar Landing Training Vehicle. Nicknamed "the flying bedstead" because of its resemblance to a four-poster bed, the LLTV was designed as a training device that approximated the experience of piloting the lunar module. Of course, nothing could duplicate the sensation of maneuvering in space and across the surface of a planet with one-sixth Earth's gravity. But the LLTV did an admirable job, according to those who flew it. Equipped with a turbofan engine and two hydrogen peroxide rockets, the craft had some stability issues. On May 6, 1968, Neil almost became a casualty of those issues.

Following an afternoon of practice landings, the pilot noticed that he was rapidly losing control of the craft and had only a few seconds to regain control before the LLTV crashed. When the vehicle made a sharp thirty-degree bank about fifty feet above the ground, the astronaut wisely decided to eject. With that, the flying bedstead smashed to the ground and burst into flames. The rocket-powered ejection seat sent Armstrong far above the flames, and he was able to steer his parachute away from the crash site. He bit into his tongue as the seat separated from the LLTV—but amazingly, that was his only injury.

Still, it was a sobering reminder that, despite the fame and adulation that accompanied the word *astronaut*, Neil was still just a test pilot—with all the hazards inherent in that profession.

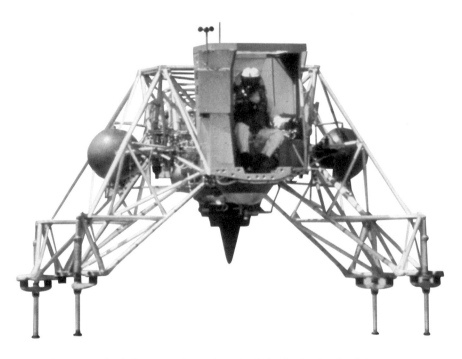

Neil Armstrong lands the LLTV—the machine that helped train pilots for flying the lunar module. It was an awkward and unpredictable piece of equipment, as Armstrong learned the hard way.

CHAPTER 11

Launch Time

Lift off! We have lift-off!
—Mission Control

Jan Armstrong was worried. The weeks and months of intense training were taking their toll on Neil. Although the moon landing was the ultimate test flight, none of Armstrong's previous tests had had so much riding on them. No flight in history had ever been discussed, dissected, and anticipated like the first lunar landing. No flight in history had ever captured a global audience the way this one would.

"Neil used to come home with his face drawn white, and I was worried about him," Jan remembered. "I was worried about all of them." Ten- and twelve-hour days were the norm, as Armstrong worked in the simulators and studied detailed step-by-step guides to the mission. He did not want or need outside distractions, such as the popular sport of trying to guess who would leave the lunar module first, thus becoming the first human to set foot on the moon.

Who Would Be First?

In reality, Armstrong didn't especially care whether he climbed out first or whether it was Buzz Aldrin, his partner in the LM. Aldrin, however, had made it known that he did want to be the first man to scramble down the LM steps and press his boot into the dusty soil of the moon. Much of his reasoning was solid, but NASA—and particularly Deke Slayton—had to consider many factors in deciding who would leave the most famous footprint in history.

In his autobiography, titled *Deke!*, Slayton argued that the decision boiled down to seniority. "It bounced back to me and I told Buzz I thought it should be Neil, on seniority. I felt pretty strongly that the ones who had been with the program the longest deserved first crack at the goodies. Had Gus been alive, as a Mercury astronaut, he would have taken the first step. Neil had come into the program in 1962, a year ahead of Buzz, so he had first choice."

Although Buzz Aldrin, seen here in his *Apollo 11* spacesuit, wanted to be the first one out of the lunar module, Armstrong was chosen because of seniority.

Additionally, the powers at NASA had already agreed that the first man on the moon should be someone with a personality similar to the famous pilot Charles Lindbergh's. "Lindy" had never taken the fuss and fanfare about his 1927 transatlantic flight to heart. Indeed, he tried in vain to live a quiet, anonymous life—especially after his baby son was kidnapped and killed in 1932.

Chris Kraft, director of Mission Control, had proposed that the first man on the moon needed to be someone like Lindy, with little ego (or, more accurately, with the polish and control born of supreme self-confidence)—someone who would not succumb to the lure of international publicity; someone who would take it all in stride and would understand that the mission came first. Neil had proven over the years that he was the man for the job.

And so, despite several newspaper articles that had prematurely trumpeted "Aldrin to be First Man on the Moon," it was Armstrong's name announced at a NASA press conference

A pioneer in flight, Charles Lindbergh set an example of humble, quiet strength. NASA wanted the first man on the moon to have a personality reflecting the low-key "lucky Lindy."

on April 14, 1969. Buzz Aldrin accepted NASA's decision, but he wasn't happy about it.

With the who's-out-first debate resolved, the three astronauts of *Apollo 11* could focus on final preparations for their flight. But Armstrong eventually summed up his perspective on the issue when he joked to the *Christian Science Monitor* newspaper, "What I really want to be, in all honesty, is the first man back from the moon!"

A "Dress Rehearsal"

Apollo 9 achieved its primary goal of successfully testing the recently completed LM in Earth's orbit. NASA could now breathe a little easier that all three major components—the Saturn V booster; the command/service module, which would take the astronauts into lunar orbit; and the LM, which would transport the astronauts to the surface of the moon—had been proven in space.

Likewise, the *Apollo 10* mission in May 1969 provided a "dress rehearsal" for the moon landing. *Apollo 10*'s LM would fly to within eight miles of the lunar surface before returning to the command module.

Beginning with *Apollo 9*, NASA had relaxed its prohibition against naming the spacecraft. The *Apollo 9* team had christened their command module *Gumdrop* and their LM, *Spider*. For *Apollo 10*, the crew paid homage to America's most popular comic strip, naming the command module *Charlie Brown* and the lunar module *Snoopy*. As fun and descriptive as these were, everyone knew that the *Apollo 11* mission would require more dignified nicknames.

Armstrong, Aldrin, and Collins discussed the naming options with the same seriousness as the more life-and-death aspects of their mission. They finally settled on *Columbia* for the command module and *Eagle* for the lunar module.

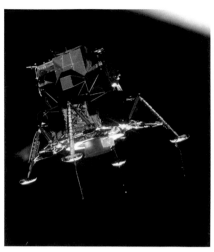

An odd-looking but strangely noble little spacecraft, the lunar module, or LM, allowed two astronauts to travel to the moon's surface.

Preparing for Launch

After spending Fourth of July weekend 1969 with his family, Armstrong went into **quarantine** with the other two astronauts so they wouldn't pick up any bugs that might delay the launch. Everyone was acutely aware that the eyes of the world were on this mission. The three astronauts held a nationally televised press conference on July 14, but they spoke from a private room and were interviewed over closed-circuit television by journalists.

Jan Armstrong brought her sons Ricky and Mark to Florida for the launch. She planned to view it from a friend's boat in the Banana River, several miles away.

At 4:10 on the morning of July 16, Deke Slayton tapped on the door to the astronauts' quarters and summoned them to their

The Command/Service Module

The command/service module—sometimes called the command module, the CSM, or the command *and* service module—was half of the mechanical team that would carry men to the moon's surface. The command/service module would take the three astronauts from Earth's surface into lunar orbit; the LM would carry two astronauts down to the moon's surface and return them to the command/service module, which would be orbiting the moon with one lone astronaut aboard. Together, these two machines were known as the Apollo spacecraft.

But the CSM was also made up of two parts: the command module, which housed the crew and the equipment and the service module that carried electrical power, propulsion, and storage space. Before the astronauts reentered Earth's atmosphere, the service module would be **jettisoned**. Of all the parts sitting on the launchpad—the Saturn V, the command/service module, and the lunar module—only the command module was intended to return to Earth intact.

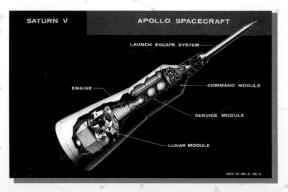

Only the very top of the massive Saturn V rocket would make the trip all the way to the moon—and even less of it would actually return to Earth. This photo shows where the lunar module was stored, as well as the cramped quarters where the two-man crew would spend their journey to the moon and back.

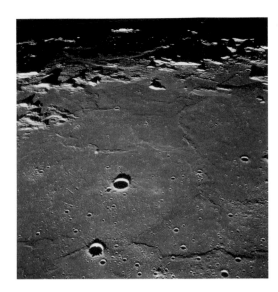

Apollo 10 flew within 8.4 nautical miles of the lunar surface and took some spectacular photos of the gray and barren landscape.

last Earth-bound breakfast for a while. Steak and eggs had become the traditional meal on launch day, with a strong cup of coffee to wash it all down. Then began the lengthy and often uncomfortable process of outfitting the astronauts for space travel. The bulky space suits were just the finishing touch. The astronauts needed to be outfitted with numerous layers of material and gadgets—including unpleasant devices that would allow them to use the bathroom in space without making a mess. Remember, in zero gravity, everything floats!

As the astronauts climbed into the NASA van that would take them to their spacecraft, thousands of anxious spectators crowded the beaches, streets, and yards in the Cape Canaveral/Cocoa Beach area. In the viewing stands, a mile from launchpad 39A, sat U.S. congressmen, governors, and special guests, including Armstrong's brother, Dean, and his sister, June Hoffman.

Back in Wapakoneta, Ohio, Neil's parents were watching their television set. They were hardly alone. All over America, parents

Launch day captured the attention of everyone in America. The viewing stand hosted dignitaries including Vice President Spiro T. Agnew, far right, along with former president Lyndon B. Johnson (center) and his wife, Ladybird.

were waking their children. Families were huddled in front of the "boob tube" waiting for the historic moment when *Apollo 11* would leave Earth and begin its journey to the moon.

Liftoff

At 6:52 a.m., Armstrong stepped into the *Columbia* and took the left seat. In the Apollo spacecraft, as in airplanes, the commander flew "left seat" while the copilot flew "right seat." Mike Collins settled into the right seat position, as the man who would be flying the command module while Buzz and Neil were on the lunar surface. Buzz, the LM pilot, took his place in the middle.

All the months of training, frustration, and preparation had come down to this one moment. In a matter of seconds, the historic journey would begin. The astronauts were confident but hardly relaxed. Even they could not know with certainty how the trip would end. Would they come back triumphant? Would they come back at all?

At roughly 9:32 a.m., the giant engines of the Saturn V rocket sprang to life and the towering spacecraft summoned all of its 7.6 million pounds of thrust and slowly lifted off the pad.

"Lift off! We have lift-off!" came the announcement from an exuberant Mission Control in Houston.

Throughout the launch, Armstrong's hand had stayed near the abort handle. If there was any sign of trouble, he was to twist the handle and trigger the escape tower that would blast the command module out of harm's way. And trouble could come in many forms. The crew of *Apollo 11* was sitting high atop what amounted to a 363-foot-tall bomb, loaded with kerosene, hydrogen, and oxygen. A major malfunction could result in a massive fireball that would be seen all over central Florida.

But Armstrong soon reported to Mission Control that the launch was a smooth one. "That Saturn gave us a magnificent ride," he told Houston.

Back on Earth, Jan and the boys prepared to head back to Texas—but not before chatting with the press about the launch. Exhausted and eager to get home, Jan remained positive for the public: "It was a tremendous sight. I was just thrilled."

Up in space, Neil and his crew were getting down to the business of flying a spaceship. It would take almost three days for them to reach the moon and begin their lunar orbit.

On the night of July 19, the astronauts slept fitfully. It was impossible not to be edgy and alert. Only sixty-six years earlier, Orville and Wilbur Wright had tested a small, odd-looking flying machine over the sands of Kitty Hawk, North Carolina. The next morning, Armstrong and Aldrin would be testing a small, odd-looking flying machine over the dusty surface of a dark and airless world. There would be no second chance.

Apollo 11 launches into a crisp blue Florida sky, as thousands crowd the streets and beaches to watch.

CHAPTER 12

The *Eagle* Has Landed

Houston, Tranquility Base here. The Eagle has landed.

Mike Collins was now, officially, the loneliest person in history. Never had a human being been more cut off from his fellow man than Collins was as Armstrong and Aldrin climbed into the LM, undocked, and began their descent to the lunar surface. All alone inside the command module, Collins was 250,000 miles from Earth and sixty miles above his traveling companions.

Descending to the Moon's Surface

Inside the gangly little LM, Aldrin and Armstrong manned the controls with quiet tension, eyeing the buttons, switches, and lights that spread out before them, leaning forward occasionally to take some visual cues from the rapidly approaching moon.

The two astronauts weren't seated as they piloted the peculiar little spacecraft. In fact, they couldn't have sat down if they'd wanted to. The LM was designed so its passengers would stand throughout their short flight from

The *Apollo 11* command and service module is photographed through the window of the lunar module on its way to the moon's surface.

the larger command module to the moon's surface. It may not have been the most comfortable way to travel, but it solved several problems, the biggest of which was weight.

The designers of the LM knew that the machine needed to be light so that it could be carried into space atop a massive Saturn V rocket, along with the command and service module, a three-man crew, and two thousand tons of rocket fuel. Original conceptual sketches had included large windows as well as seats for the astronauts. In later designs, the Grumman Aircraft engineers who were building the LM discovered that seats and windows would exceed the weight limitations and could make the difference between success and failure.

So the designers substituted two small triangular windows and agreed that making the astronauts stand during the flight to the moon's surface wouldn't be such a bad thing. After all, the engineers reasoned, the astronauts would likely be pumping **adrenaline** as they slowly maneuvered down to the moon. The two space travelers would be focused and tense; kicking back in a chair would be the furthest thing from their minds! Plus, human legs are designed to be efficient shock absorbers. If the moon landing was a bit bumpy—as it surely would be—the astronauts would handle it better in a standing position.

Neil snapped this casual photo of his lunar module pilot, Buzz Aldrin.

And so it was that Neil Armstrong from rural Ohio and Edwin "Buzz" Aldrin of Montclair, New Jersey, stood alone in the *Eagle* while Mike Collins patiently circled the moon in the *Columbia*, waiting to take all three of them safely back to Earth.

The Risk of Exploration

At this point, no one was taking anything for granted. In fact, Collins's training had included how to return home solo if Armstrong and Aldrin were lost somewhere between the command module and the moon. It was not something Collins wanted to think about—especially as he sat alone in the orbiting command module and eyed the hostile, ashen landscape some sixty miles beneath him—but he was a professional and he had to be ready for anything.

Mike Collins studies the *Apollo 11* flight plan during simulation training at Kennedy Space Center.

The two LM passengers were also well aware of the risks of the moon shot. In fact, they had frankly discussed the possibility that they might not make it through the mission alive.

But the astronauts of *Apollo 11* understood what all explorers know: that discovering new horizons and divergent paths cannot be done without risk. Someone has to be willing to step forward and assume that risk. Someone has to be willing to offer his or her own life to move humankind to a new vantage point.

A Decision Under Pressure

As Armstrong and Aldrin maneuvered the LM closer to the moon, they stayed in radio contact with Mike Collins in the command module and with Mission Control in Houston. Fellow astronaut Charlie Duke was serving as capcom (capsule communicator) at Mission Control for this mission. It was Duke's job to relay information between the astronauts and the technical experts in Houston who were monitoring every aspect of the LM's descent.

In an instant Aldrin and Armstrong's concentration was broken by the scream of an alarm inside the tiny LM.

"Program alarm," Armstrong announced to Mission Control. "It's a 1202."

More than a quarter million miles away, the guys in Houston were scrambling to determine the seriousness of a 1202 alarm. So many things could go wrong on this complex mission, and it would only take one problem to wreck the landing—or worse.

Flight Director Gene Kranz paced tensely as his staff researched the origins of a 1202 alarm. Twenty-six-year-old Steve Bales, the guidance officer for that day, was consulting with his associates Gran Paules and Jack Garman. The Mission Control computers were frustratingly slow at spitting out any usable data, but Bales and Garman were certain they had an answer.

"Give us a reading on the 1202 program alarm." Neil Armstrong's voice carried just a hint of urgency, detectable even across the void of space.

Again Kranz raised an eyebrow in the direction of his guidance officer. Steve Bales's voice cracked slightly as he announced with as much certainty as he could muster in the nineteen seconds he'd had to make a decision, "We're go on that, flight"—meaning that the alarm was not anything serious.

Flight Director Eugene Kranz would make the final decision on whether conditions were suitable for the LM to actually land on the moon's surface.

The controllers had agreed that the alarm was a minor glitch—just a matter of the computer system "thinking" it was overloaded. Years later, Bales would acknowledge that, while certain of his decision, he was *only* certain in the context of their Earth-bound simulations. Everything happening up on the moon was completely new. All bets were off and, for the moment at least, the future of the American space program rested on nineteen seconds of consideration by a twenty-six-year-old and a twenty-four-year-old.

"We've got you . . . we're go on that alarm," Charlie Duke radioed to the LM.

"Roger," Armstrong replied and turned his attentions back to the complexities of landing the LM.

Seconds later the alarm blared again. And once more Houston reassured the astronauts that all was well.

As the LM drew closer to the lunar surface, Armstrong could see that their anticipated landing site was peppered with huge rocks. In order for the duo to return safely to the command and service module, the *Eagle* had to land on a flat, smooth area. Armstrong saw no such terrain from his tiny window.

It was time to override the automatic landing system and manually fly the *Eagle* to safer terrain. But with sixty seconds of fuel remaining, it would take total concentration and two cool heads to pull victory from the jaws of disaster.

Landing the *Eagle*

Aldrin recited the computer readouts as Armstrong quietly maneuvered the LM over the rocky terrain.

"Thirty seconds," came Charlie Duke's urgent reminder from Houston. Dust from the moon powdered up around the feet of the LM as it sank toward a flat surface that Armstrong had finally spied from the *Eagle*.

"Contact light!" Buzz called out, signaling that the LM's feet were almost on the ground. After a few seconds, Charlie Duke radioed back, "We copy you down, *Eagle*."

A second of silence hung tensely in the air before Neil Armstrong radioed back the historic words, "Houston, Tranquility Base here. The *Eagle* has landed."

The *Apollo 11* mission patch with an American bald eagle settling on the moon's surface visually reflects the success of the *Eagle's* landing.

"Roger Tranquility. We copy you on the ground," the capcom radioed back. "You got a bunch of guys about to turn blue. We're breathing again. Thanks."

And then, for a brief moment, there were no polished professional engineers manning the panels at Mission Control; there was only a crowd of excited kids, whooping, hollering, and slapping one another on the back.

Across America, people were similarly celebrating and breathing sighs of relief. Most adults and many children would forever recall where they were and what they were doing the moment that man first landed on the moon.

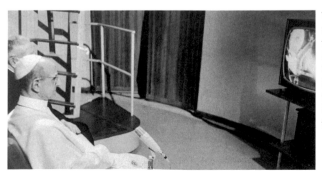

The whole world was fascinated by the moon landing, including Pope Paul VI, shown here in his summer villa watching the first humans walking on the moon.

Tranquility Base

Neil Armstrong named *Apollo 11's* landing site on the moon's surface Tranquility Base. The base is located in the southwest corner of a lunar plain called the Sea of Tranquility (often referred to by its Latin name, *Mare Tranquillitatis*). Of course there's no real sea there, because there's no water on the moon, only powdery gray soil. The unofficial location names were immortalized during the moon landing, but prior to the LM setting down on the moon's surface, only fellow astronaut Charlie Duke knew what Armstrong intended to call the landing site.

"Magnificent desolation" was Buzz Aldrin's description of the lunar surface. This photo of the Sea of Tranquility captures it beautifully.

For Armstrong and Aldrin, it was a much quieter, more personal moment. Their individual journeys had been even longer and more complex than the 250,000 miles of darkness they had just crossed. Now they would be forever and uniquely connected by the incredible reality that they were the first two human beings to land on the moon.

If they reflected on the magnitude of their situation, it was brief. There was much to be done before the singular moment when they would step out of the LM and explore this gray and hostile world.

CHAPTER 13

We Came in Peace

That's one small step for man; one giant leap for mankind.

The surface of the moon had long been a mystery. For many years, children—and even some adults—believed that the moon was made of green cheese! Scientists knew better, but even they weren't completely sure of its true consistency. Some feared that the astronauts might sink down when they stepped onto the surface. There were theories much wilder than that, including a Chinese legend that the moon was inhabited by a beautiful girl and her companion, a jade rabbit. Japan and Korea also had their own folklore featuring lunar rabbits. And of course, there were still those who wondered what kind of little green men would show up to greet Armstrong and Aldrin.

After three hours of securing the LM, the two astronauts asked Mission Control if they could venture out onto the moon. The flight plan had factored in four hours of rest, but it hadn't factored in the adrenaline rush fueled by finally landing on the lunar surface. Sleep was the last thing the two explorers wanted to do now.

George Méliès's 1914 silent film *A Trip to the Moon* captured early fascination with the concept of space flight. This image from the movie depicts the Man in the Moon with a rocket in his eye.

Dressing for EVA

The EMU/MMU (extravehicular mobility unit/manned maneuvering unit) was like a self-contained spacecraft that the astronauts would have to wear before they could wander around the moon's surface.

Since space is a near vacuum and there is no air to breathe, an astronaut's EVA clothing must have breathable air, temperature control, moisture, radiation protection, and a communications system. It must also be strong enough that it can't be torn if the astronaut is struck by space debris. The Gemini space suits were based on the suits used in the X-15 program. The G3C and G4C suits were worn for all Gemini missions but *Gemini VII.*

The G3C had six layers of nylon and Nomex, a flame-resistant fiber. The suit had removable combat-style boots, along with a full-pressure helmet (containing earphones and microphones) and detachable gloves.

The GC3, worn for the *Gemini III* mission, was replaced by the GC4, which was very similar but came in two different styles. Both had layers of Mylar to protect against radiation and to retain heat, but the commander's suit had removable boots, while the pilot's version had integrated boots and a detachable sun visor that clipped onto the helmet.

Today's NASA space suits are called EMUs or extravehicular mobility units. They are much stronger and more advanced than the Gemini and Apollo models. They are very much like flexible spaceships that fit around the astronaut!

Mission Control okayed the earlier time for the EVA (extra-vehicular activity), and the two astronauts donned the portable life support systems (PLSS) that would protect them from the harsh environment of the moon.

One Small Step

At approximately 2:56 **Greenwich Mean Time** (GMT), Neil Armstrong squeezed out of the LM and started down the ladder. Americans were glued to their TV sets watching the grainy black-and-white transmission from more than a quarter million miles away. Before climbing out of the LM, the astronauts had deployed a Westinghouse camera from the LM. The camera hung in a position that allowed it to capture the historic steps. Afterward, the camera would be detached from its mount, placed on a tripod, and used by the astronauts to capture further images from the first EVA.

As Neil reached the bottom rung of the ladder, he paused. Then he set his foot onto the powdery soil of the moon.

"That's one small step for man; one giant leap for mankind," he said. His boot imprint was clearly visible on the ground, thus laying to rest all concerns that the surface of the moon was anything but solid.

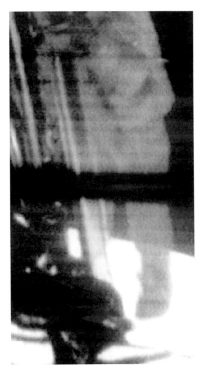

A camera mounted on the LM captures Neil Armstrong's historic first step onto the moon's surface.

There has been much discussion over the years about Armstrong's first words on the moon's surface. He has stated that what he intended to say—what he thought he did say—was "one small step for a man . . ." However, even Armstrong admits that the "a" is not audible in the Apollo recordings. Whether he said it or not, America and the world knew what he meant and embraced the statement wholeheartedly. Few phrases have been more repeated, **parodied**, and appreciated in the history of the world.

Shortly after Armstrong's historic step, Aldrin climbed out of the LM and surveyed the gray landscape. "It's beautiful," he said, catching his breath. "Magnificent desolation."

The most famous footprint in history: Neil Armstrong's boot in the dusty lunar soil.

Using a seventy-millimeter camera, Neil Armstrong photographs Buzz Aldrin stepping out of the lunar module.

Attending to Business

Armstrong set up the camera so that it would capture images as the two astronauts went about their business. He also unveiled the plaque attached to the portion of the LM that would remain on the moon and read it the audience back on Earth: HERE MEN FROM THE PLANET EARTH FIRST SET FOOT UPON THE MOON, JULY 1969 A.D. WE CAME IN PEACE FOR ALL MANKIND.

He and Aldrin also planted an American flag into the soil and offered a crisp salute.

There were other smaller items that the astronauts would leave on the lunar surface. These included an *Apollo 1* patch paying tribute to the astronauts lost in the launchpad fire—Gus Grissom,

The plaque left on the moon's surface by the Apollo astronauts, which states, in part: WE CAME IN PEACE FOR ALL MANKIND.

Buzz Aldrin poses next to the flag that symbolized America's victory in the space race. Because there was no wind on the moon, the flag had to be wired so that it would stretch out and be visible.

Roger Chaffee, and Armstrong's former neighbor and close friend, Ed White. Also left on the dusty soil were the medals of two Soviet cosmonauts, Vladimir Komarov, the first man to have died during a space mission, and Yuri Gagarin—the first human in space, who tragically died in a plane crash while training for his second space mission.

After almost an hour of hopping across the moon's surface and getting accustomed to one-sixth the gravitational pull of Earth, Armstrong and Aldrin were advised that someone wished to speak with them. President Richard Nixon greeted them from the Oval Office of the White House.

"This certainly has to be the most historic telephone call ever made," he said. "For one priceless moment in the whole history of man, all the people on the Earth are truly one—one in their pride in what you have done, and one in their prayers that you will return safely to Earth."

Following the historic transmission, the two astronauts focused on collecting soil and rock samples and setting up several experiments, one of which would test whether the moon had a core structure similar to Earth's. *Apollo 11*

Among the items that were left on the lunar surface was an *Apollo 1* mission patch, a tribute to the crew who gave their lives in the quest for the moon.

would return to Earth with over forty-six pounds of soil and rock samples. Once back on Earth, the basalt (volcanic-like) rocks were judged to be somewhere around 3.7 billion years old. As old as that was, later Apollo flights brought back samples even older!

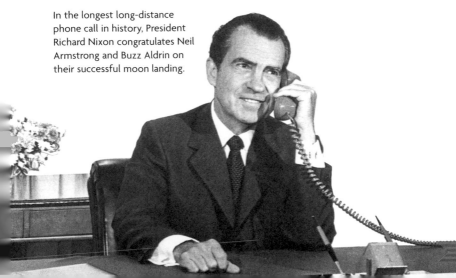

In the longest long-distance phone call in history, President Richard Nixon congratulates Neil Armstrong and Buzz Aldrin on their successful moon landing.

Studying Moon Rocks

Armstrong and Aldrin brought back over forty-six pounds of moon rocks for scientific research purposes. Knowing more about the geological history of the moon helps us better understand the evolution of Earth.

Scientists who studied the moon rocks in depth unlocked many long-standing mysteries, including the moon's age and where it came from. They were able to lay to rest speculation that the moon's craters had been formed by volcanoes. Instead, the astronauts discovered that the craters were hills of rocks that had piled up when asteroids and meteorites struck the lunar surface. It was also determined that the moon was once covered with an ocean of molten rock that eventually cooled and formed a crust. These findings helped lead scientists to a theory called the Giant Impact Hypothesis, which suggests that more than four billion years ago, Earth was struck by a huge object, roughly the size of the planet Mars. When the object hit, it exploded. Pieces of it flew into orbit around Earth, eventually joining together to form what we know today as the moon.

Buzz and Neil finished all the tasks on their EVA and headed back into the *Eagle*, where they ate some dinner and tried to sleep. They were exhausted, having started their day some eighteen hours earlier, but sleep came slowly. The LM was cold, the seats provided for rest time were not made for comfortable snoozing, and the astronauts were still burning off the day's adrenaline. Oddly, one of their biggest sleep distractions came from the bright glow of Earth shining into the cabin. They were truly among the very few people who could claim to have been awakened by "the Earth in my eyes!"

In addition to their physical discomforts, the two astronauts had to be wondering whether the reunion with the command module would go as smoothly as the launch, the flight, and the landing had. After such a successful mission, it would be a tragedy to mess up on the return trip.

Returning to the Command Module

After a fitful sleep, Neil Armstrong and Buzz Aldrin prepared the LM for its reunion with the *Columbia*. The bottom half of the *Eagle* would remain on the moon's surface, while the top half blasted away from Tranquility Base and up toward the orbiting Mike Collins.

The launch from the moon's surface went surprisingly smoothly. Aldrin looked up in time to see the blast from the rocket engine knock over the American flag they had planted. But, all scenarios considered, they could not have asked for a more flawless departure.

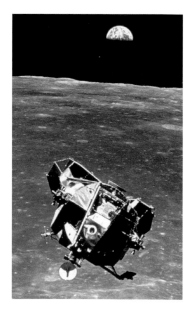

After docking with the command module, the astronauts opened the LM hatch and waited for Collins to do likewise on his side. Once he had, the tired and dusty explorers climbed back into the vehicle that would take them

Astronaut Mike Collins captures the lunar module on its journey back to the command module from the face of the moon.

home. Although there was still plenty that could go wrong, the major nail-biting portions of the journey were now behind them.

Mike Collins recalled his own joy at once again seeing his crewmates alive and well. "The first one through is Buzz, a big smile on his face. I grab his head, a hand on each temple, and am about to give him a big smooch on the forehead, as a parent might greet an errant child." Then, slightly embarrassed by his own emotion, Mike opted for a firm handshake instead. The trio spent a few moments laughing, joking, and sharing their giddy relief before getting down to the business of heading home.

The trio spent a few moments . . . sharing their giddy relief before getting down to the business of heading home.

Heading Home

The astronauts offered physical proof that the toughest part of the journey was behind them by catching a full eight and a half hours of sleep on the first night of their flight home. It was a far cry from the nervous catnaps that had punctuated their moonward journey.

The last nerve-racking segment of the trip would be reentry and the LOS (loss of signal) that occurred during the spacecraft's fiery descent toward Earth. Although there was no indication of any breech in *Apollo 11*'s heat shield, it was still one of those needles-and-pins moments when everyone held their breath and waited for the crackle of a radio transmission and the reassuring sound of an astronaut voice.

The heat shields protected the spacecraft from the intense heat of reentry. A damaged shield could spell disaster for the astronauts. Many years later, in February 2003, NASA would learn this bitter lesson as the space shuttle *Columbia* broke up during reentry due to several heat shield tiles that had been damaged during liftoff. All seven members of that shuttle crew were killed.

For this mission, the heat shields remained strong and intact, and at roughly 11:45 a.m. "Houston time" (Central Daylight Time), the gang at Mission Control watched with relief as three huge orange-and-white parachutes billowed out from the speeding command module, slowing its descent into the approaching choppy waters of the Pacific Ocean. At 11:51, the heat-scarred space capsule struck the water forcefully, jarring all three of the tightly belted astronauts.

"Everyone's okay. Our checklist is complete. Awaiting swimmers," came Neil Armstrong's last official transmission from the command module *Columbia*.

Half an hour later, the astronauts were plucked from their waterlogged vehicle by navy frogmen and placed into a bobbing life raft to await the helicopter that would take them to the USS *Hornet* aircraft carrier.

Once the astronauts were safely in the helicopter, they headed to the *Hornet*, where the mood was decidedly festive.

Splashdown! After completing the most famous journey in history, the *Apollo 11* capsule bobs across the top of the ocean as navy divers assist in retrieving the three astronauts.

Thousands of cheering sailors crowded the deck. Standing on the bridge was President Nixon, flanked by Secretary of State William Rogers and NASA administrator Thomas Paine. It was a homecoming like no other.

In Quarantine

Unfortunately, there was little time to enjoy the celebration. The astronauts were quickly shuttled into a quarantine chamber, where scientists would test and study them for twenty-one days. Because no one knew what kind of bacteria or germs the astronauts had picked up on the moon, everyone who encountered them had to wear protective clothing. Only after being declared free of space germs would the astronauts be able to return to their families.

Still, they were home. Finally back on "the good Earth." With five months to spare, NASA had indeed fulfilled John F. Kennedy's challenge to "place a man on the moon and return him safely to Earth before this decade [the 1960s] is out."

Armstrong was quick to credit the successful mission to the hundreds of thousands of Americans who had studied, built, and tested the components for the spacecraft. Even today, decades later, it is tough to summarize the incredible marriage of teamwork and technology that made possible the first moon mission and the

Back on Earth, the *Apollo 11* crew went immediately from the command module to a quarantine area. There they received a visit from President Richard Nixon, who congratulated them on their historic mission.

subsequent Apollo flights. It puts things in perspective somewhat to realize that even the cheapest, most stripped-down computer available in stores today has hundreds of times more processing power than the computers that took *Apollo 11* to the moon.

Although Aldrin and Collins hated the isolation and boredom of their quarantine, Armstrong was happy for the peace and quiet. It seemed like it had been forever since he could relax and savor the silence.

But if any of the trio thought they were coming home to reclaim a "normal" life, they were sadly mistaken. Astronaut Jim Lovell had spoken to the crew just prior to reentry. He summarized the global hysteria over the successful mission by cautioning the space travelers: "I just want to remind you that the most difficult part of your mission is going to be after the recovery."

And it was true. All three astronauts—and especially Neil Armstrong—would never again be *just pilots* or *just astronauts* or even *just men*. They were legends. They were explorers on par with Christopher Columbus, destined to be remembered for as long as humankind endured. It was a burden none of them had fully anticipated, and each man dealt with it in his own personal way, and with varying levels of success.

The moon landing was not simply an American achievement. The whole world reveled in the adventure, as seen in these newspaper headlines from countries around the globe.

CHAPTER 14

Rocket Man

I'm not the man they think I am at all . . .
—*Elton John*

Shortly after the *Apollo 11* mission, some officials at NASA suggested sending the astronauts and their families to a dude ranch for relaxation. At that, aviation pioneer Harry Combs hit the roof and told them, "The public would tear them to shreds. They needed somewhere quiet and secluded where they could just be themselves."

Combs volunteered his sprawling Sleeping Indian Ranch in Colorado. Neil, Jan, and the boys enjoyed a week of total seclusion where they were able to rest, fish, and take long walks or horseback rides through the rough and beautiful high country. It would be the beginning of a close personal friendship between Armstrong and Combs.

When the Armstrongs left the Combs' ranch in 1969, they headed out into the media circus that would define a large portion of the rest of their lives. Headlines, parades, screaming fans, and the inevitable autograph seekers were a constant reality.

The *Apollo 11* crew came home to a grand welcome. This August 13, 1969, ticker-tape parade in New York City may have been the biggest celebration ever held in the Big Apple.

A Friendship of Mutual Respect

When Harry Combs began a careful study of the Wright brothers, resulting in a definitive book on their efforts to achieve flight, it was Armstrong whom he credited as the inspiration. "I had always thought of the Wrights as a couple of bicycle mechanics who got lucky," Combs recalled. "Neil knew better and he urged me to find out more about the science behind their invention. He sent me a beautiful two-volume set of the Wright brothers' letters and memoirs. It was the beginning of my own incredible journey as I began to discover what geniuses these two men truly were."

The end result of that journey was the brilliant and insightful *Kill Devil Hill: Discovering the Secrets of the Wright Brothers.*

When Combs established a research center at the National Aviation Hall of Fame in 2002, he talked at length to the research director about possibly naming the center for his buddy Neil. After much thought and discussion, he scrapped the idea, admitting that "Neil would just try to talk me out of it and I don't want to put him in that position."

It was an incredibly short period of time between the boxy-looking Wright flier, pictured above in 1909, and the massive Saturn V booster that sent the astronauts 250,000 miles from Earth.

Life After *Apollo 11*

Armstrong handled superstardom with grace and dignity. He turned down movie offers, product endorsement opportunities, and myriad love letters he received from women seeking the dubious fame of snagging the first man on the moon as their own. He and Jan bought a farm in Lebanon, Ohio, about fifty miles south of Wapakoneta. Mark and Ricky attended school in Lebanon, and Armstrong resigned from NASA in 1971, opting instead to serve as a professor of engineering at the University of Cincinnati.

"Professor" Armstrong emerges from his office at the University of Cincinnati, where he taught engineering following his retirement from the astronaut corps.

At the height of the early space program, two rock stars each released songs that summed up the public adoration for the men known as astronauts. Elton John produced "Rocket Man" in 1972, and David Bowie released "Space Oddity" in 1969. If ever a line in a song described Neil Armstrong's ambivalence toward being a global celebrity, it was the observation in "Rocket Man" that "I'm not the man they think I am at all . . ."

Although Armstrong is proud of his achievements, he remains to this day an intensely private person. Neil Armstrong has lived as quietly as his fame will allow, devoting his professional energies to teaching and to research projects. His leisure time has been directed toward charitable work, including support for the Boy Scouts and fund-raising drives for Easter Seals and for a new YMCA built on the outskirts of Lebanon.

He continued to fly and even test piloted jets for Harry Combs's Gates Learjet Corporation. In 1979, he set an altitude record of fifty-one thousand feet for a business jet.

Armstrong handled his superstardom with grace and dignity.

He left his teaching position at UC in 1980 and took board positions at several companies in the Cincinnati area. He "returned to space," at least in spirit, in 1984 when he accepted a position on the National Commission on Space (NCOS), which was formed to help America define its space exploration objectives for the twenty-first century. But any plans the commission developed became incidental on the morning of January 28, 1986, when America watched in horror as the shuttle *Challenger* exploded against the backdrop of a brilliant blue Florida sky.

Following the *Challenger* disaster, Armstrong was named vice chairman of the Rogers Commission, which investigated the causes of the accident. As Frank Borman had with the *Apollo 1* investigation, Armstrong offered an astronaut's perspective and helped to uncover the explosion culprit, a defective O-ring on one of the solid rocket boosters.

After almost two decades of successful space missions, America was reminded of the dangerous nature of space travel when the shuttle *Challenger* exploded in the Florida sky.

In 1987, Jan Armstrong opened a travel agency in a small town called Twenty Mile Stand, just south of Lebanon. But the external pressure from years of living in a fishbowl had taken its toll on the couple's thirty-eight-year marriage. In 1989, Neil and Jan quietly divorced. Jan later described the breakup as the result of two very different personalities that grew more different with the passing years. Less than a year after the divorce, Neil endured the pain of losing both parents within a few months of each other. A year after that he suffered a heart attack while skiing with friends in Colorado.

A New Wife

It was a grim period in Armstrong's life that was substantially brightened when he met Carol Knight in 1992. Knight, a widow with two teenage children, turned out to be the perfect complement to Neil's introspective nature. Their friendship blossomed into romance, and the two were married in 1994. Carol easily embraced the challenges of being Mrs. Neil Armstrong, not even objecting when the media inevitably identified her in photos as Janet. "That's fine. It's not about me," she said.

Following his 1989 divorce from Janet, Armstrong met Carol Knight in 1992. Two years later, Carol and Neil were married.

"She is a humdinger," Harry Combs announced. "A perfect fit for Neil. She really changed his

life and gave him a new beginning."
Other friends agreed that Neil's and
Carol's personalities complemented
each other ideally. Janet had
acknowledged that such was not the
case for her and her ex-husband—
and she was not alone. Few who knew Neil could claim to
understand what made him tick.

Few who knew Neil could claim to understand what made him tick.

Accepting His Place in History

In Neil Armstrong's 2005 authorized biography, *First Man: The Life of Neil A. Armstrong,* author James R. Hansen suggests that Armstrong is finally at peace with himself and his place in history, that he is "perhaps happier than at any other time in his life."

The former astronaut continues to fly whenever he has an opportunity, and he still savors the quiet beauty of glider flight.

Armstrong isn't mobbed by the public as regularly as he once was. Still, at the 2003 Pioneers of Flight Homecoming in Dayton, Ohio, he had to be escorted into the convention center through a back hallway to avoid the crowds hoping to catch a glimpse of— or even touch—the famous flier. It was an amazing testament to Armstrong's enduring impact.

More than thirty-five years after his triumphant voyage to the moon, Neil Armstrong prefers to use his quiet voice to champion worthwhile causes and to advocate for more and better space research. He wears the mantle of "first man on the moon" with style, if somewhat reluctantly.

Between 2000 and 2005, the authors of this book were among the officials at the National Aviation Hall of Fame who were fortunate to visit with Neil Armstrong on many occasions. When you're talking to Neil, you forget that he is a living legend. It is only much later that you pinch yourself and realize: *I was talking to the first man on the moon!*

Neil Armstrong's name will forever be linked to the dangerous, awe-inspiring, and historic journey that gave Americans a taste of what is truly possible with teamwork, vision, and the pioneering spirit that has always fueled our curiosity about what lies just beyond the horizon.

On July 20, 1999, the *Apollo 11* astronauts gathered at Kennedy Space Center in Cape Canaveral, Florida, to celebrate the thirtieth anniversary of the moon launch. Pictured from the left are Mike Collins, Neil Armstrong, and Buzz Aldrin.

NASA After *Apollo 11*

Moon exploration got bolder in the missions that followed *Apollo 11*. Here Eugene Cernan, "the last man on the moon," takes the lunar rover out for a spin.

After the moon landing, the space program itself endured some troubled times as America's fascination with space travel began to wane. Only six more lunar flights took place after *Apollo 11*. One of those, *Apollo 13*, never made it to the moon due to an explosion in the service module en route. The mission was deemed a "successful failure" because NASA teamwork helped to bring the three astronauts on board home alive.

Apollo 17 would be the final moon mission. Although many believed that men from Earth would be exploring Mars by the end of the twentieth century, such a thing has not happened. Nor has NASA ventured back to the moon even once in the intervening years. In fact, visitors to the Cape Canaveral area of Florida can occasionally catch glimpses of the rusting hull of a Saturn V rocket, identical to those that once stood proudly on launchpad 39A ready to deliver men safely to the moon and home again.

Glossary

adrenaline—a hormone that is released into the bloodstream in response to high-stress or physically exhilirating situations.

aerodynamics—a study that focuses on how an object responds to the flow of air over its surface.

aileron—the hinged surface that is used to control the aircraft during a roll; along with the rudder pedals, it helps the plane to turn.

astronomer—one who studies objects and matter outside the earth's atmosphere.

diagnostics—systems or machines designed to find the cause of a condition or problem.

g-force—a force acting on a body as a result of acceleration or gravity.

Greenwich Mean Time—once used for scientific purposes, Greenwich Mean Time (GMT) is the local time at the 0 meridian passing through Greenwich, England; it is the same everywhere. GMT is no longer used in scientific endeavors.

hangar—a building where aircraft are kept.

jettison—to throw or eject an object from an aircraft, spacecraft, or ship.

lunar—referring to the moon. From the Latin *luna*, for "moon."

maneuverability—the ease with which something can be moved and controlled.

midshipman—a low-ranking commissioned officer in the U.S. Navy.

mission patches—small cloth patches that symbolize the goal of a specific NASA mission.

oscillation—a vibration, shudder, or shaking sensation.

parodied—imitation for comic effect or ridicule.

photo reconnaissance—the act of exploring an area by shooting pictures and studying them for information.

propellant—something, such as an explosive charge or rocket fuel, that propels or provides thrust, thus moving an object forward or upward.

quarantine—to place an individual or object in isolation (away from others), usually to contain a possible serious disease.

rocket plane—an airplane propelled wholly or primarily by a rocket engine.

velocity—the speed and direction at which something moves.

zero gravity—a condition in which the apparent effect of gravity is zero, as in the case of a body in free fall or in orbit.

Bibliography

Books

Aldrin, Edwin, Neil Armstrong, and Michael Collins. *First on the Moon*. Boston: Little, Brown and Company, 1970.

Barbree, Jay, Howard Benedict, Alan Shepard, and Donald K. Slayton. *Moon Shot*. Atlanta: Turner
    Publishing, 1994.

Cernan, Eugene. *Last Man on the Moon*. New York: St. Martin's Press, 1999.

Chaikin, Andrew. *A Man on the Moon: The Voyages of the Apollo Astronauts.*
    New York: Viking Penguin, 1994.

Collins, Michael. *Carrying the Fire: An Astronaut's Journey*. New York: Farrar, Straus and Giroux, 1974.

Dunham, Montrew. *Neil Armstrong: Young Flyer*. New York: AladdinHansen, 1996.

James R. *First Man: The Life of Neil A. Armstrong*. New York: Simon & Schuster, 2005.

Kramer, Barbara. *Neil Armstrong: The First Man on the Moon*. New Jersey: Enslow Publishers, 1997.

Rau, Dana Meachen. *Neil Armstrong*. Children's Press, 2003.

Slayton, Donald K. *Deke!* New York: Tom Doherty Associates, 1994.

Zimmerman, Robert. *Genesis: The Story of Apollo 8*. New York: Dell Publishing, 1998.

Web Sites

"Neil A. Armstrong Biography," NASA. www.nasa.gov

"Being the First Man on the Moon, Ed Bradley Talks to Neil Armstrong About Fame, Family and *Apollo 11*,
    July 2, 2006," CBS News. www.CBSnews.com

Pearlman, Robert Z. "NASA Honors Neil Armstrong with Moon Rock Award," April 18, 2006,
    collectSPACE. www.collectspace.com

"Neil Armstrong, Astronaut/Test Pilot," National Aviation Hall of Fame. www.nationalaviation.org

"Technical Air to Ground Voice Transmission from Apollo 11 Mission, July 1969," NASA.
    http://history.nasa.gov

"Special Message to the Congress on Urgent National Needs. May 25, 1961," JFK Link. www.jfklink.com

"Flight Day Five: A Man on the Moon," SPACE. www.space.com

"*Freedom 7* 1st American into Space," The Ultimate Space Place. www.thespaceplace.com

"We Will Bury You! November 26, 1956," Time. www.time.com

"Good Landing and Excellent Landing," Airline Pilot Forums. www.airlinepilotforums.com

Interviews

Howard Benedict (former AP reporter covering the space program, co-author of *Moon Shot*, and
    former executive director of the Astronaut Scholarship Foundation), interviewed by Tara Dixon-Engel,
    Cocoa Beach, Florida, March 2000, July 2000, and December 2001.

Harry Combs (aviation pioneer and friend of Neil Armstrong), interviewed by Tara Dixon-Engel,
    Phoenix, Arizona, April 2002; Dayton, Ohio, July 2002 and July 2003.

Transcripts

NASA, *Johnson Space Center Oral History Project*, Oral History Transcript. Neil A. Armstrong.
    Interviewed by Dr. Stephen E. Ambrose and Dr. Douglas Brinkley, Houston, Texas, 2001.

Musical Score

John, Elton. "Rocket Man." Rocket Record Company. UK, 1972.

Source Notes

The following list contains citations for the sources of quoted material found in this book. The first
and last few words of each quotation are cited and followed by their source. Complete information on
referenced sources can be found in the Bibliography.

Abbreviations Used:

APF—Airline Pilot Forums Web site

ATG—*Apollo 11* Technical Air to Ground Voice Transcripts, July 1969

DK—*Deke!*

FM—*First Man: The Life of Neil A. Armstrong*

HB—Howard Benedict interview

HC—Harry Combs interview

PAGE 110 *"The public . . . be themselves."* HC
PAGE 111 *"I had . . . truly were."* HC
PAGE 111 *"Neil would . . . that position."* HC
PAGE 112 *"I'm not . . . at all"* RM
PAGE 114 *"That's fine . . . about me."* FM, pg. 645
PAGE 114 *"She is . . . new beginning."* HC
PAGE 115 *"perhaps happier . . . his life."* FM, pg. 646

Image Credits

About the Authors

Tara Dixon-Engel is the former director of the Harry B. Combs Research Center at the National Aviation Hall of Fame (NAHF); **Mike Jackson** is executive director emeritus of the NAHF. The duo left the NAHF facility in 2004 to become national chairs of the Operation Welcome Home celebration for America's Vietnam veterans. They have since founded the American Veterans Institute, based in Tipp City, Ohio, which honors and supports veterans at the grassroots level. They are currently working to establish the American Veterans Hall of Honor and Research Library in Indiana. They have previously authored *The Wright Brothers: First in Flight* (Sterling Publishing, 2007) and *Naked in Da Nang* (Zenith Press, 2004), as well as two award-winning videos on D-day and the Vietnam conflict.

Index

Discover interesting personalities
in the Sterling Biographies® series:

Marian Anderson: *A Voice Uplifted*

Neil Armstrong: *One Giant Leap for Mankind*

Alexander Graham Bell: *Giving Voice to the World*

Christopher Columbus: *The Voyage That Changed the World*

Jacques Cousteau: *A Life Under the Sea*

Davy Crockett: *Frontier Legend*

Frederick Douglass: *Rising Up From Slavery*

Thomas Edison: *The Man Who Lit Up the World*

Albert Einstein: *The Miracle Mind*

Benjamin Franklin: *Revolutionary Inventor*

Matthew Henson: *The Quest for the North Pole*

Harry Houdini: *Death-Defying Showman*

Thomas Jefferson: *Architect of Freedom*

John F. Kennedy: *Voice of Hope*

Martin Luther King, Jr.: *A Dream of Hope*

Lewis & Clark: *Blazing a Trail West*

Abraham Lincoln: *From Pioneer to President*

Rosa Parks: *Courageous Citizen*

Eleanor Roosevelt: *A Courageous Spirit*

Franklin Roosevelt: *A National Hero*

Harriet Tubman: *Leading the Way to Freedom*

George Washington: *An American Life*

The Wright Brothers: *First in Flight*

Malcolm X: *A Revolutionary Voice*